GUTSY
FAITH

Hard Conversations with God

by

Jeff Edmondson

BEACON HILL PRESS

OF KANSAS CITY

Copyright 2006
By Jeff Edmondson and Beacon Hill Press of Kansas City

ISBN-13: 978-0-8341-2262-8
ISBN-10: 0-8341-2262-6

Cover Design: J.R. Caines
Interior Design: Sharon Page

Library of Congress Cataloging-in-Publication Data

Edmondson, Jeff, 1966-
    Gutsy faith : hard conversations with God / by Jeff Edmondson.
        p. cm.
    Includes bibliographical references.
    ISBN-13: 978-0-8341-2262-8 (pbk.)
    ISBN-10: 0-8341-2262-6 (pbk.)
    1. Christian life. I. Title.

    BV4501.3.E365 2006
    248.4—dc22

                                                    2006013592

10 9 8 7 6 5 4 3 2 1

GUTSY
FAITH

CONTENTS

To my boys, Logan and Brady, who inspire
me to live with a gutsy faith everyday.

And to my oldest brother, Jordy,
who planted the seed that grew into the book.

WHERE GUTS BEGINS

Scriptural Basis: *Read John 11:1-43.*

1

"Don't be an idiot," he told me. "How can you be sure you're doing the right thing? You're leaving a prime position with a bright future. To do what? Go work at a tiny church in backwoods Virginia? I really think you should reconsider your decision, Jeff. Churches are notorious for paying their youth pastors nothing and expecting them to live on faith and hand-me-downs. Is that what you want for you and your new wife?"

The phone line remained silent for a long time while I contemplated how to respond. No doubt my oldest brother was hoping his words of wisdom had really sunk in. In truth, there was only one sentence he'd said that had caught my attention: *How can you be sure you're doing the right thing?*

How could I be sure? What was it that made me so certain that leaving my career as an officer in the Air Force and then moving me and my soon-to-be wife across the country to accept a youth pastor's position at half my current salary was *the* right thing? Exactly how did I know that's what God was calling us to do?

I reassessed how I'd come to the decision. I had spent months praying about the possibility of taking the position. I'd searched the Bible for answers. I'd sought the counsel of close friends. All seemed to confirm to me that the position in Harrisonburg, Virginia, was where God was moving us.

But beyond all this, I just knew this was the way to go. From the moment I was first asked to consider the position, I knew it was the right thing to do. In my gut I knew. I had heard God speaking to my heart time and again, telling me this was His will.

My oldest brother, Jordy, was right in one respect. From a sheer economic standpoint I could hardly refute him. It was crazy to resign my stable Air Force officer's commission for a position as a youth pastor at a small church. After all, how many youth pastors were let go annually, simply because the small church they served couldn't afford to keep paying their measly salaries? Too many. That was the side to this decision that made me nervous. Yes, it was nuts. But even with the fear of financial ruin hanging over my head, I couldn't escape it. That was my calling.

Then I considered Jordy's spiritual condition. At that time he wasn't living for the Lord. Although my siblings and I had all been raised in the church and taught to love and obey God from an early age, at that time in his life, my oldest brother was living far away from the Lord. And that's what angered me. I was almost indignant that he would even question whether I knew what God was calling me to do. My decision was crystal clear to me, and I would not let the threat of financial difficulty bring doubt into that decision.

I chose my words carefully. "Thanks for your advice, Jordy," I responded. "But when you are living for the Lord, in a daily, deep relationship with Him, speaking to Him day and night, and when you are involved in the ministry of a local body of believers, then I will listen to you. Until that time, I'll thank you to keep your advice about my life calling to yourself, and I'll accept my own counsel instead." The uncomfortable silence on the line settled on us again. I waited for his response.

"All right. I guess I'll talk to you later," Jordy stated.

"Fine. Bye." I hung up the phone, fuming. How dare Jordy, who had no relationship with God, question my decision? As the moments passed, my anger abated. I knew he wasn't trying to irritate me with his questions. Jordy, because of his protective nature, was simply trying to look out for me, attempting to prevent me from making what appeared to be a bad decision. But he had left me questioning how sure I really was.

A week later I called Jordy to see how he was doing. We chose not to dredge up the previous week's conversation. We both respected each other too much. He respected my freedom to choose my own course for my life. I respected his right, as my brother, to question if I really knew what I was doing. We both loved each other too much to hold a strong disagreement against each other.

Three months later my newly wedded wife and I moved to Harrisonburg, Virginia.

Years later I knew it was the best move I ever made in my life.

— — — — — — —

Over a decade since then, that conversation remains frozen in my memory. I even remember what I was doing as I talked to my brother: I was sitting on my couch on my day off, watching a late September Colorado rain shower blow over the front range and begin sprinkling on my outside patio. My beloved pug, Thor, was nestled down beside me having a good nap.

It was a formational moment in my life. I praise God that my brother Jordy had the guts to ask me those questions, because that conversation was the genesis of what has become the book you are now holding. The exchange we had that day launched me on a stream of thought, research, and Bible study in a quest to find out exactly how we can be sure of God's voice in our lives. From that moment on my life took on a new shape.

Several months ago I was visiting Nashville on business

and I had dinner with Jordy and my sister-in-law, Dawn. They asked me to tell them about the book I was working on. I smiled and reminded him of our phone conversation so many years ago. For the life of him, Jordy couldn't remember it at all.

"Well, whether you remember it or not, it drove me to find the answers to exactly how we can know God's will in our lives," I said.

Jordy forked the plate of sesame chicken sitting in front of him. Having since settled his relationship with God, he smiled and asked, "So, what's the answer?"

"Faith," I said, "Gutsy faith." We spent the next hour discussing exactly what a no-holds-barred, open-communication-based, gutsy faith relationship with God was all about. As we talked, our broccoli beef, sesame chicken, and fried rice grew cold.

While the waiter boxed up our left-over food, Jordy said, "Well, I might not remember that phone call, but I sure am glad I asked what I did that day."

"Me too," I agreed.

FAITH . . . AND GUTS?

Do you understand what it means to have guts? Aside from the obvious definitions dealing with internal organs, *The American Heritage Dictionary* gives the following definitions to the word "guts": "guts: 1) One's innermost being. 2) The inner working parts. 3) Courage; fortitude. 4) Nerve; audacity. 5) To remove the essence, or substance. 6) Deeply felt."

When a person is described as having guts, we generally mean that person is very brave, able to take on any situation without batting an eye. We often see him or her as fearless or unshakable.

If we described a person as having a gutsy faith, we might think of him or her in the same way: Through prayer, nothing shakes a person with a gutsy faith. But just as the word "guts" has various meanings that can apply to various situations, couldn't it mean much more to say a person had a gutsy faith? Couldn't it also apply to someone who knows the inner workings of his or her soul—a person who might know how to respond to any given situation based on the knowledge of what God might be doing in his or her inner being?

When we look at an individual's depth of faith from a holistic, life-changing perspective, the kind of gutsy faith we will be exploring has roots in all of the definitions we've listed as it correlates both to God and to our relationship with Him.

Yes, sometimes just answering God's call can be a harrowing experience. Obedience can bring frustration, fear, and turmoil. Sometimes, even when we know we're in the center of God's will, it would just be so much simpler to give up, to quit. Sometimes living up to what God calls us to means all that we know, all that our lives represent, and all that we have come to believe in will end. In such circumstances, it's clear that having faith to move forward would take a lot of intestinal fortitude—guts.

But I am of a mind that having guts in our faith is so much

more than dealing bravely with making difficult decisions. I think that having a strong, unshakable faith takes guts in a variety of ways. We will explore those in this book.

I also fully believe that having that kind of faith is something a person develops. We aren't born with it. Some will develop guts in their faith easier than others, but in the end, we are all capable of having a gutsy faith.

As you move through this book, I challenge you to record your responses. At the beginning of each chapter I've included a large block of Scripture that I challenge you to read. No doubt God will begin speaking to you through His Word about the kind of guts the particular characters in the block of Scripture possessed, and what it took for them to get there. Write those thoughts down.

And at the end of each chapter I have included "thought questions" for you to answer. The thought questions are designed to help you really dig into the deeper meaning of each chapter and how this deeper meaning applies to your life. I encourage you to record your answers, to journal your thoughts as you progress through these pages.

You may even want to take this journey with a friend or two. Open vulnerability with a trusted friend not only is good therapy but also helps you work through what God might be saying to you. And true accountability is one of the best ways to grow a gutsy faith.

So, are you ready to develop a gutsy faith? I assure you, this isn't going to be the easiest read you've ever had. It will likely be challenging. It's going to require blatant honesty from you in order to reach that gutsy level of faith in God. If you *are* ready, let's begin.

THOUGHT QUESTIONS

■ What does it mean to you to have a gutsy faith?

■ Do you think of yourself as a person with a gutsy faith? Why or why not?

■ Name at least five people in the course of your life whom you see as having a gutsy faith.

■ What characteristics do these people possess that you would like to see developed in your life?

■ Are those characteristics key to their gutsy faith?

■ If so, why do you think that is the case?

■ If not, why do you want to develop those characteristics in your life?

■ What reasons do you see for why you lack those characteristics?

YES, NO, OR LATER?

Scriptural Basis: *Read John 11:1-43.*

She didn't understand at first. How could she have a *mass* in the back of her throat? Her dentist *had* to be mistaken. She simply had a toothache that he needed to attend to. How could a supposed *mass* be related to her current dental need?

"Barbara," her oral surgeon said, "I'm going to schedule you for a biopsy on this. If it's a tumor, it may be pressing on the nerves in your gum line. That may be the reason for the pain you're experiencing. It could be nothing, but we need to make sure."

"Dr. Dasher, couldn't the pain just mean I need a root canal?" she said, trying to reassure herself, as if a root canal was a less dismal prospect. The words "tumor" and "biopsy" caused levels of uncertainty to rise up in her mind, the reality of which she wasn't sure how to handle.

His lips thinned in a sort of smile. The absurdity of her statement was not lost on him. He had heard similar objections before. "Possibly, but I won't know without some X-rays. And either way, that lump in the back of your throat needs to be looked at. We've got to rule out all the possibilities just to be sure."

Two weeks later the biopsy results revealed the worst, a malignant tumor that had been growing for quite some time. The doctors suspected the tumor had metastasized, spreading throughout her neck and upper chest cavity. Surgery no longer was a distant prospect, it was now a certainty, and it would happen soon.

Barbara and her family were devastated at the news. Cancer? But how? This wasn't supposed to happen to a person like her. She was a mother of four, a teacher, a God-fearing woman. Wasn't God supposed to protect her from these kinds of things? What would happen if the procedures didn't work? What would happen to her husband and children if she died? Who would take care of them? The questions were endless and anguishing.

For her, the only answer was to pray. The Sunday before the surgery, the church gathered around Barbara, laid hands on her, anointed her with oil, and asked God for a miracle, to cure her of this destructive disease that could easily rob her of her life.

When the surgeons went in, they were surprised that the tumor came out easily. Strangely enough, the mass seemed to be encapsulated by tissue. As they progressed with the surgery, exploring her chest cavity for escaped tendrils of the cancerous growth, they could find nothing. They were stumped. How could this be? The presurgery tests had revealed that Barbara's malignancy had spread. Yet, aside from the tumor that they had already removed with no difficulty at all, they could find nothing.

God had answered prayer.

One more chance was all he had. If he failed this time, it was over, and all his hopes, dreams, and plans for the future would end abruptly. Bart had spent the past four years preparing for pilot training, his ultimate aspiration to become a pilot in the United States Air Force. Through college he'd been at the top of his class of ROTC cadets. He'd worked hard to wrap up his private pilot's license. After graduation and his commissioning as an officer, he attended the Air Force's Flight Screening Program where he'd also excelled, finishing at the top of his group. Following the Flight Screening Program he transitioned directly to pilot training. The first month of the yearlong program consisted of eight-hour days full of bookwork and academics. And yet again, Bart surpassed his fellow pilot candidates.

But when he'd started his second month in pilot training,

everything changed. Despite his past experience in flying, and despite his never having experienced motion sickness, halfway through his first training jet flight, Bart unexpectedly threw up. Unperturbed, he chalked it up to nerves and excitement and chose to not let it bother him. After all, half of the other pilot candidates had similar experiences.

The next day was a repeat of the first. Bart got sick again. Lieutenant Bettner, his instructor pilot, encouraged Bart to not let it distract him. Many pilots went through this same phenomenon their first week or so in the jets. It would pass.

But it didn't. For the next month, every day that he climbed into the training jet cockpit, Bart got sick. And they'd tried everything. Drugs. Relaxation therapy. They'd even sent him through a weekend of "air sickness control" training. Nothing worked. He still got sick every flight.

At the end of each day, Bart would retire to the sanctuary of his room and spend the next hour in prayer. *God, I know You didn't bring me this far with this dream just to drop me,* Bart would say each day. *You've orchestrated this whole thing. I trust You, God, that You will give me a sickness-free flight tomorrow.*

Three days prior to his scheduled solo flight, Bart drove in complete silence to the base. The pressure of today's flight bore down on him like a deep-sea diver at the bottom of the ocean. Regulations required that chronically airsick pilot candidates have two successful, sickness-free days of flights at least two days prior to their solo flight. Therefore, if Bart got sick today, it was over. He would be washed from the pilot training program.

The odds that he would have a successful flight today were stacked against him. His heart cried out for God to work wonders, to change the course of what had been happening. He couldn't imagine what life held for him if being an Air Force pilot was not in his future. It was his "God-given" dream. Every waking minute of the past five years had been spent preparing for that dream. It hadn't been an easy road. He'd simply trusted God to work out all the details to get him to this point. And true to form, God had taken care of everything. How could God do all that only to allow the dream to come crashing down now? God wouldn't allow the dream to die, would He?

That day Bart's flight was perfect until he entered the landing pattern. As he entered the downwind leg, he was forced to turn over control of the plane to his instructor pilot. Though his stomach convulsed several times, Bart managed to control himself just long enough to retrieve an airsick bag from his flight suit pocket, remove his air mask, and get it around his mouth.

It was over. God's answer to all of Bart's prayers for deliverance was a no.

━ ━ ━ ━ ━ ━ ━

For a long time Cheri and her husband had prayed for a baby. Yet none came. She often blamed herself, wondering what sin she had committed to be stricken barren. Each month she beat herself up, begging for forgiveness and for God to give her a child. But for her and her husband it seemed that pregnancy was simply what happened to every other couple they were acquainted with.

She and her husband had tried almost everything. They changed their personal habits and daily rhythms just as all the fertility books suggested. Their doctors ran tests and prescribed drugs. They kept ovulation and temperature charts. They tried personal advice from their friends and family. Yet Cheri remained barren.

She could not understand why God would not give her a baby. She loved kids. She would be a good mother. Every night the news reported case after case of child abuse. Why would God allow people who seemed to disdain the fact that they were *saddled* with children to continue to have them, when she and her husband remained childless? Hadn't they sacrificed enough? Her husband was a pastor. They had given their hearts and souls to the work of the Church. Couldn't God grant this one request? Unfortunately, having a baby remained an elusive fantasy.

After five heartbreaking years, God moved them to Kansas City. Cheri found a new doctor who ran even more tests. The results showed that it was physically impossible for her to become pregnant without serious medical intervention. The news was crushing. They did not have the financial wherewithal to afford the treatments that the doctors recommended. Cheri's dream to give birth to a baby now seemed to be a true impossibility.

But, against the medical findings, the next month, without any medications or treatments, Cheri became pregnant. Nine months later she gave birth to a baby boy.

After such a long period of time, God had finally answered Cheri's prayers.

Three different stories, each true, each with a different answer to the prayers that were offered up. Barbara received a resounding yes. Bart, a no. Cheri was given a yes, but much later than the original request. I can attest to the validity of each of these testimonies as they are each very close to my heart. You see, Barbara is my mother, Cheri is my wife, and I am the Bart character (Bart's actually a shortened version of my middle name). With great clarity I recall each incident.

I remember the hopelessness I felt when my mother announced her cancer. In the late 1970s, doctors had fewer options and a less-than-perfect record of treating and curing the disease. I remember my brother and me lying in our beds at night, consoling each other, wondering what we were going to do *when* our mom died of cancer. I recall the day of the surgery, driving down to Shand's Hospital in Florida, nervous that the doctors would exit the operating room with more bad news to heap on what we were already struggling with. We all marveled when the doctors actually brought back a cautious, yet highly optimistic prognosis. We all knew that God had performed a miracle.

When Cheri and I were handed the news that we couldn't get pregnant naturally, we were miserably shaken. We knew we had the option to adopt, and we actually were moving down the road with that alternative. I remember the deep agony I felt as my wife cried all the way home, a 45-minute drive. After years of trying to conceive and then finding out it was impossible, our hopes were demolished. But then just one month later, to our astonishment, we discovered that the impossible isn't all that impossible for God. Cheri became pregnant. And nine months later, our first child entered our home.

And I'll never forget the despair I experienced when my dreams of aviation magnificence came crashing down around me. I remember questioning whether God really did care for me. I couldn't believe He would not answer my passionate pleas.

My life experiences have caused me to question why God chooses to answer prayers in the manner He does. The "church" answer is that God is God, and He is free to answer our prayers in the manner that best suits His plan and His kingdom. I'm not disagreeing with that statement. I just want to know why.

Why is it that God would heal my mother of cancer, while other strong Christians never receive healing? Why did God wait so long to grant a child to Cheri and me? And while I certainly have seen God's hand at work in my life since being washed out of Air Force pilot training, did the possibility of being a military pilot have to be completely removed from me in order for God's will to be fulfilled? Couldn't He as easily have worked it all out so that I could have still flown for the Air Force, even if only for a few years?

Beyond all that, why does it seem that God grants the prayers of certain Christians almost all the time, yet for others it's as if He ignores their petitions? Have you ever wondered that yourself? When that occurs, it almost causes me to wonder if God plays favorites.

In my local congregation we have certain people we've unofficially designated as prayer warriors. They are the ones we always seek out to pray for us when we find ourselves in need. For some reason, we trust their prayers for us, as if God hears their voices above all others and grants their prayers more readily. I'm not sure that statement holds much clout from a theological perspective, but it still doesn't stop me from seeking prayer support from prayer warriors. And as it happens, God does *seem* to bless their prayers with a yes more often than not.

What about those prayers that get a no, even when the request would obviously further God's kingdom? I can't tell you the number of times I've prayed for ministry needs to be met, only to receive what appears to be a denial. Have you ever found yourself praying for one of the saints in your local congregation who is sick or dying? Have you ever received a no answer during those desperate times? Why does God allow that to happen?

THE GOD WHO ALWAYS ANSWERS

Each of us has asked those or similar questions sometime during our lives. It's human nature to do so. Humanity has a primal instinct to ask why. As children of the God of the universe, why can't He just answer yes to all our requests?

When I was a teen, I remember making the statement during a Sunday School class that God doesn't always answer our prayers. My teacher was quick to correct me. "That's not true, Jeff. God *always* answers prayer," she said. She now had my undivided attention. I was positive I must have misunderstood her. She continued, "He answers our prayers with a yes. He answers our prayers with a no. Or He answers them with a yes, but later. But He always answers prayer." I rolled my eyes at this simple and almost naive idea. It wasn't really the nugget of wisdom I thought she was going to hand me, but I chose not to argue with her.

I can't tell you why that moment in my history sticks so vividly in my mind. But I can tell you I've contemplated this theology, or rather *ideology,* since that day. In reality God does answer our prayers with a yes, a no, or a later. What other choices are there? But I can find no scriptural basis that this is how God *wants* to answer our prayers. In fact, I find blocks of biblical text seeming to contradict the yes, no, or later ideology.

So then, why do we accept it as being true?

I believe we have it all wrong. I believe that God's desire is to *always* say yes to His people. When I shared this idea with my brother Bob a number of years ago, I believe his exact words for me were, "You're crazy!" No doubt you may be saying the same thing right now.

Living a gutsy faith starts from the basis that it is never God's desire to say no to His children. Therefore, I ask you to put aside your doubts and reservations for the time being. You may have uncertainties regarding that claim, but take a small step forward toward having a gutsy faith. For the time being, count it as a fact that God doesn't really want to answer your prayer requests with a no. We'll explore this concept further as we go along. But for now, just trust me.

THOUGHT QUESTIONS

- Has God ever answered one of your prayer requests with a no? If so, what was it and what were the circumstances surrounding it?

- Has God ever answered one of your prayer requests with a yes, but later? What was the prayer request and the circumstances surrounding it?

- What about a yes answer to a prayer request? What was it and the circumstances surrounding it?

- Describe how you felt after you knew each of God's answers?

- Why do you think God answers no or later at times?

- Why doesn't God always answer our prayers with a yes?

EVERYTHING HE ASKED FOR

Scriptural Basis: *Read Matt. 14:13-23.*

The boat bobbed at the water's edge, the bow nestled two feet ashore while the stern swayed in the shallows, rising and falling with each low wave that rolled in. By the thousands, people gathered on the beach, spilling over into the rocky fields beyond the sandy banks, some wading out into the water. Sad faces, anxious faces—windows to the empty, broken lives each represented— focused on the grounded vessel, but more specifically, one of the men it carried.

Of those inside the small craft, one robust figure rose from where He was seated and slipped over the edge into the breaking tide. With quiet confidence He waded ashore and eased into the crowd, strong muscled hands clasped behind His back, a strange smile cresting His lips and a glint in His eyes. Against the throngs of people, His broad shoulders cast an imposing figure, the result of working for years in His father's construction business. Everywhere He looked there were people—old, young, feeble and dying, possessed —people with broken bodies, lives, and hearts drawn to this charismatic yet simple man, this Jesus.

They came because of what they'd heard He could do. The rumors were that He could heal the sick with a simple touch. Only a prophet great in the Lord could heal like that. And it had been quite some time since a mighty prophet of God stood among them. They'd tried everything else yet nothing had worked. They weren't going to miss their chance to be healed, to be set free.

The throngs pressed in on all sides like mighty avalanches of sweating, anxious flesh, each impatient, anxious to reach their only hope, Jesus. Today they had cast off all social status to be in His presence. Those born to luxury stood side-by-side with the destitute and forgotten. Like cattle gathering for the evening feeding, women layered in silken gowns and scented with incense jockeyed for position, rubbing and bumping up against filthy, stinking street urchins. Elite bankers, tax collectors, and lawyers crowded together with beggars, vagabonds, and prostitutes, all for the chance to be near this man.

Though thousands had gathered, with painstaking patience and that same confident smile, Jesus listened to every request, every need, every story. Jesus looked right at them, right through them, as if He knew exactly what they were talking about. He never rushed them. After listening He would say a short prayer, a simple request to His Heavenly Father. And then, always, God honored that request. The sick were healed immediately. The blind received sight, and the deaf gained hearing. Bones of the crippled knit themselves together right before their eyes. And with each person He touched, Jesus praised God.

On occasion Jesus took the healing opportunity to teach a deeper life lesson to the masses. Yet despite those periodic interludes throughout the day, Jesus never hesitated in His task. He healed them, one after another after another, each time giving all praise to His Heavenly Father, until at the end of the day He'd met the needs of everyone gathered.

Eventually the sun arced across the sky and hung low on the horizon. Jesus' disciples came to Him, urging Him to dismiss the crowds so they could grab a bite to eat. "You feed them," Jesus suggested.

Casting dubious glances between each other, they answered, "Yeah, well we only have five loaves and two fish. It's impossible to feed this many people with just that."

With one eyebrow raised Jesus responded, "Bring what you have to Me and let's see how impossible it really is." After having the crowd make themselves comfortable, He offered a simple prayer of blessing to His Heavenly Father. He tore the bread and fish into pieces, and His disciples began passing it out. He continued tearing and tearing and tearing. As the broken pieces seemed to multiply, Jesus filled baskets with the bread and fish, smiling and joking with those around Him as if this were simply business as usual. But, then, for Him it was. Once again, Jesus made a simple request of His Heavenly Father and it was granted.

The disciples fanned out among the thousands. Basket after basket, on and on, they continually served and passed out bread and fish until finally, every man, woman, and child had eaten his or her fill.

Jesus' companions reported back to Him that there was no reason to continue breaking up the food anymore. Everyone had been fed. They laid 12 baskets on the ground in front of Jesus, the leftover pieces they'd gathered up.

Tossing the bread He was holding into the nearest basket, Jesus wiped His crumb and fish oil crusted hands on His robe. He maneuvered between the baskets, eyes roving from one disciple to the next, examining, probing.

"What was that you were saying, 'only five loaves and two fish'?" The reactions were mixed. Some of His disciples had truly doubted and could not hold Jesus' gaze. A few couldn't believe what they'd seen, but they nodded their approval, gladly accepting the lesson like apprentices finally comprehending ancient lessons. The rest stood perplexed, staring back at Him, pondering who exactly this man was.

"The boat's still down at the water's edge. Why don't you guys take it across to the other side? I'll catch up with you later," Jesus told them. He glanced at the horizon. The setting sun cast fluorescent shades of scarlet and orange in the gathering clouds above. "Better hurry. There's a storm brewing." They didn't question this time. They knew better. One by one they filed past Him, silent and contemplative.

Turning to the host of people, He spoke a benediction and dismissed them as well. Slowly, like a great lumbering, frothing wave, clumps and family groups rose from where they reclined and ebbed away.

With the vast burden of the day finally off His shoulders, Jesus climbed a nearby hill. It overlooked the open body of water, and He could clearly see the silhouette of the boat as His disciples made their way toward the deep. On the other side of the hill He could clearly see the nearby towns. Lantern light flickered in the windows and spilled out through the doorways in the fast approaching twilight. The trails and roads were glutted with people heading home, busy discussing the happenings of the day. He could hear their voices dwindling in the distance, excited, laughing, renewed, changed.

Finally alone, through sighs of exhaustion, Jesus inhaled the silence. It was as if He'd been smothering and now He could finally breathe again. A cool, refreshing breeze whispered around Him. His robes fluttered.

He sank to His knees, welcoming this time. Throughout the day He'd patiently listened to each request. He'd endured the anxious crowd, tolerated their demands and attitudes. Long after others would have quit, worn out from the sheer mental strain of it all, Jesus had continued, confident in what His Father could do through Him, knowing all along this moment would eventually arrive.

On some level, everything that had happened today had importance. Everything that had transpired carried some redeeming quality in the scope of eternity. The people who'd been healed, the relationships mended, each one would never forget the day he or she was personally touched by the human hand of God. But all those moments in time paled in comparison to this one. Their importance meant nothing to Jesus if this moment would never have arrived. This was His time to be ministered to. He asked for it, and it would be granted. This was His time with His Father. He'd waited patiently for it all day long. And despite His exhaustion, despite all the burdens He'd born throughout the day, nothing would keep Him from this moment. Nothing.

▬ ▬ ▬ ▬ ▬ ▬ ▬

Ever wonder how Jesus always knew precisely what to say or do and precisely when to do it? No matter what circumstances He faced, there never was any doubt in Jesus' mind what He was going to do on a daily basis. Every hour of every day, down to the minutes and seconds, He knew exactly what His purpose was. He never worried about whether He'd offend someone or whether He'd break any human laws by His actions. He never called a committee to determine if He should or shouldn't perform a certain miracle. Jesus always knew what to do, and He always did it—swiftly, without hesitation, regardless of the consequences. How is that so?

Furthermore, Jesus never questioned whether what He

wanted to do would or wouldn't happen. Things always turned out like He said they would. He never asked God for anything that didn't unfold exactly as He'd requested. He never attempted to heal a person or perform a miracle only to have it flop. He prayed, laid hands on the person, and every time, without fail, the person was healed. There were no misgivings about what He was capable of. He didn't call for a vote, as if perpetrating a wondrous act was a democratic decision. He never worked the crowd into a charismatic frenzy. There was no hell-fire and brimstone performance, no flashes of lightning or bells and whistles. Jesus simply employed unadorned, unshakable faith with no worries, frustrations, or anxieties. Why such confidence?

If you've read through the Gospels at least once in your life, you might have noticed God never told Jesus no. Nor did God ever say, "I'll answer that request at another time, Jesus." God's response to His Son was always instant, always yes.

Reading through this chapter's Scripture passage you see that having just received the heartbreaking news that His cousin, John the Baptist, had been beheaded, Jesus did the only natural thing for Him. He found a sanctuary away from the crowds and spent restful, quality time with His Heavenly Father. What else could He do at a time like that? Communion with the Father was all that mattered. It was where He received renewal and strength. And since He knew the tasks He faced in the near future, the best way to deal with difficult news was to curl up in His Father's comforting arms and rest.

HE POINTED TO THE FATHER

Throughout the day, with the pressure of the crowd weighing on Him, Jesus never forgot His place. Though this particular passage doesn't go into detail regarding what Jesus actually did that day, throughout Scripture Jesus gave credit to God the Father when healing anyone. He always pointed to God. Even though He was God in the flesh, Jesus never allowed others to think He was more powerful or more important than His Father. He knew His job was to glorify God, and He always did. On the particular day described in Matt. 14:13-23 it's hard to believe Jesus would have acted any differently. He pointed people to the Father all day long.

Then, before turning five small loaves of bread and two measly fish into an impromptu banquet that served thousands, what did He do? He paused to give thanks to His Father, asking God to bless this paltry meal in a way those people would never forget. And true to form, God answered His Son's prayer.

When the day came to an end, when the crowds were all gone and Jesus was by himself, once again He did what came naturally. He spent quality time with His Father. Not because He *had* to or out of compulsion. Jesus sent everyone away because He couldn't wait to be alone with God. He was anxious to put the day's business behind Him and simply relax with His Dad. It was prime time, quality time, love time. It was finally relationship time.

For anyone who's ever been in a deep relationship, there are times when you know exactly what the other person is thinking, even without speaking. A situation arises, you exchange glances, and you know what's going through the other person's mind. You don't have to ask. You just know because of the intimacy you share. That kind of knowledge doesn't come coincidentally. It only comes after years spent together—sharing, loving, experiencing, talking.

Confidentially, I tend to be more of a devious type. My wife, Cheri, chooses to call me downright ornery. On the other hand, Cheri tends to be a rather demure and quiet type. While in public settings, I love to whisper in her ear embarrassing comments, just to get her to blush. Somehow, I crave the reaction. I generally just want to get her to laugh. By now in our marriage, she knows me so well that she can look at me during those settings, read my face immediately, and usually she'll point her index finger right at me, with one eyebrow raised, and mouth the words, "Don't!" Equally, I also know those times when she really means it, or whether I can push forward with my crack. We just know each other. We know each other's signs. We know each other's personality. We know what to expect.

It was exactly the same with Jesus and His Father. Only this relationship was far more intense and personal than any of us could ever comprehend. Their relationship, their intimacy, was such that Jesus knew every minute what the Father was thinking. He would do whatever His Father asked of Him, no matter what. That was why Jesus never had to question what God wanted Him to do. That was why there were no miracles that flopped. As a result of Jesus' immeasurable love and appreciation for His Father, He faithfully obeyed what the Father wanted Him to do. And when Jesus, out of unswerving obedience, asked the Father to grant His requests, the Father always gave Jesus everything He asked for.

"Everything?" you may ask. "What about in the Garden of Gethsemane?"

Yes, even then. We will talk about the Garden of Gethsemane in much more detail later. But trust me when I say, even then, the Father *always* gave Jesus everything He asked for.

THOUGHT QUESTIONS

■ Do you think it was possible for God to answer Jesus with a no? Why or why not?

■ If God always answered Jesus' requests with a yes, do you think it's possible for Him to answer all your requests with a yes? Why do you think so?

■ In this chapter's block of Scripture, why do you think Jesus sent the disciples ahead of Him while He dismissed the crowds on His own?

■ When you've reached the end of a long, stressful day, what do you do to escape?

■ Do you think the kind of intimate relationship Jesus shared with the Father is equally possible for you and God? Why or why not?

■ What would it take to have that kind of relationship?

"DON'T WANT TO SAY NO"

Scriptural Basis: *Read Luke 11:1-10.*

4 Simon was tired, exhausted. It had been another extended, busy day. The family store had done brisk sales all day, as they had been doing now for weeks. He pondered the reason behind their vigorous sales. Could it be that someone was spreading good news about newfound health benefits deriving from eating his family's decades-old recipe? He smiled inwardly, knowing that was unlikely. He took great pride in his business and the bread they baked, but in truth both were unremarkable. Simon chalked it up to an improving economy.

Though he hated the Roman occupation, the soldiers did bring plenty of gold with them, and they were very free with it. He would not complain. After all, it had been some time since their small family shop had done the level of business they were doing lately. He would gladly take the additional income and capitalize on it. His family of seven had spent every day lately baking and selling as fast as they could.

But the current success did have its price. It seemed as if they were all at each other's throats. The children would never raise their voices at him or their mother. But he noticed that they were all snapping at each other on a regular basis. And Simon had little time or interest in being a referee. He had caught himself being short with the children and with his wife, Miriam. He took no pride in that fact. The short tempers were simply a result of sleep deprivation. There never seemed to be a time of rest these days. Bake the bread. Sell the bread. Bake the bread. Sell the bread . . . Each day, well before the eastern skies reddened and the sun spilled over the horizon, he and Miriam would rise and heat the stone ovens. The children would stir shortly after to begin their chores. Before any of them sat down to a modest breakfast, the morning's supply of loaves—now double what it was just three weeks ago—had to be formed and set aside to rise. They would then work all day, until long after the sun had set. And after the last customer was gone, the family would finally sit down in the one-room dwelling to a hard-earned dinner. They all toiled together, taking advantage of the surplus in sales, knowing that it wouldn't last forever. They would put the additional profits away in savings for less lucrative times. Future security was important.

They just seemed too busy to worry about the everyday pleasures and graciousness that kept them sane. Extended fatigue always yielded thorny results. As with the work, together they would endure each other and be thankful that God was blessing their small business. Together they would rest when they could, taking full advantage of the weekly Sabbaths. Together they would weather these minor, daily hindrances of foul attitudes.

At least rest had finally come for them all today. The dinner utensils were all cleaned and put away. Everything was prepared and set aside for tomorrow's business. The nightly story from the Torah had been recited, and the children were now resting soundly on their sleeping mats. Miriam had settled. The doors were secured. The oil lamps extinguished.

Simon reclined his head and soaked in the sounds, the rhythms of his family. The baby nestled to his wife's breast, occasionally making suckling sounds, slowly nursing for one last day's meal. His two boys lying next to each other, alternately breathing in and out deeply, in a nocturnal cadence of slumber. His oldest daughter lying next to her mother, still trying to find a comfortable position as was her nightly routine. His younger daughter on her mat just beyond, motionless, already sound asleep. He smiled. Life was busy these days, grueling to be truthful. But his family was worth the minor, temporary stumbling blocks. He would do all he could to make a better life for them.

His mind finally quieted, his body drained, and he was just dozing off when a loud rapping sounded on the door. Startled, awake and sitting up, he searched the darkened interior, hesitating, listening to see if his weary family had been awakened. In the dim light he saw his wife's head raised, a protective arm now wrapped around the baby. His daughter stirred and sat up, her blanket wrapped around her. Her eyes, wide in the dim light, like beacons, searching his face for reassurance that this intrusion was not bad tidings. His boys remained undisturbed, deep in their slumber.

Quickly, he vaulted to the nearby door. "Who is it?" he barked as loud as he dared, allowing his annoyance to be apparent, yet minding his volume so as not to disturb those family members who'd remained asleep.

"Simon, it is Isaac," came the answer.

Simon relaxed somewhat, relieved at least that it was not Romans. "What is wrong? Why have you come at this hour?"

"Forgive me, my old friend, but I need bread."

Simon exhaled frustration, bitterness. Could this nocturnal intruder not come during the day? Eleven hours of daylight and he could not show the courtesy to come during a decent hour.

"My family and I are in bed," he said. "Come back tomorrow." He turned to go back to his sleeping mat when the knocking came again.

"Isaac, go away or I will summon the authorities," Simon threatened, knowing he would do nothing of the sort.

"Simon, I would come back tomorrow, except I am in desperation. An unexpected traveling party has just arrived at our home, and we have nothing for them to eat. Please, you must help me. I only need three loaves of bread. I would be eternally shamed if I did not feed them a decent meal after their long journey."

Simon considered his friend's predicament. It truly would be dishonorable for his friend not to feed his guests. He cast a quick glance at his family, Miriam's eyes boring into him, imploring him to end the disturbance quickly. His sons now fidgeted where they lay. His family needed their sleep. If he ignored Isaac, Simon was certain he would not go away. Even though the disturbance at this hour was almost unforgivable, Simon felt compelled to help. He could not allow his friend to go away and risk shame. And the fact that he had come at such a late hour surely meant Isaac was in a desperate situation. There were still loaves of bread left from the day's batch, and it was really no effort to retrieve them for the man. He *had* to help him.

Isaac knocked at the door again. "A moment," he remarked through the closed door. "I will give you what you want. Only do not wake my family any further with your noise. I will be right with you."

In no time Simon had retrieved the three requested loaves and slipped them through the door. Isaac happily paid him extra for each loaf as a peace offering for disturbing the sanctuary of the family's nightly rest. Simon lay back down on his mat, tucking the small sack of coins below him for safekeeping until the morning.

It had been a long, profitable day. But for now, it was finally time to rest.

——— ——— ——— ——— ——— ——— ———

Context is everything where literature is concerned. Without knowing the context from which any particular sentence is drawn, the sentence itself may or may not have meaning. Or when seen by itself, a sentence might take on a completely different meaning.

If I were to tell you "Joe is dead," you might assume I was referring to a friend or loved one named Joe. Or Joe might be my dog. If you overheard me say that to someone, without knowing the context of the conversation, you might wonder all manner of things. Unless you heard the whole conversation, you just wouldn't know exactly what's going on.

Scripture is the same way. Unless the reader knows the full context of the passage he or she is reading, it truly is difficult for him or her to understand the full extent of what God wants to communicate through His Word. Unfortunately, most Christians don't have a firm grasp of ancient Hebraic culture and so often miss key insights into Scripture simply because they miss subtle clues hidden in the cultural context.

TEACH US TO PRAY

If you were to read this chapter's focus Scripture passage, without knowing what was going on before or after it, you could easily miss the richness of what's being communicated. In the Scripture passage, Jesus is spending time in prayer, yet again conversing with His Father, aligning His will with God's. While He's doing that, one of the disciples comes to Him and asks if He will teach them how to pray.

Luke's version of what we know as the Lord's Prayer records Jesus as saying,

> *Father,*
> *hallowed be your name,*
> *your kingdom come.*
> *Give us each day our daily bread.*
> *Forgive us our sins,*
> > *for we also forgive everyone who sins against us.*
> *And lead us not into temptation* (Luke 11:2-4, NIV).

To be honest, I'm rather partial to Luke's rendition of the Lord's Prayer. It's simpler. It's to the point. Luke cuts to the chase of what Jesus was trying to teach His disciples. When we notice in the context that just before He shared this, Jesus was in prayer himself, verifying He knew what God wanted Him to do, we gain a little more insight into what He wanted His team to understand.

While there are many interpretations that can be made from Jesus' words, here's my paraphrase of what Jesus was saying to them:

> *Father,*
> *You're holy, and everything associated with Your name is*
> > *holy.*
> *May everything that builds Your kingdom happen as You*
> > *see fit.*
> *Meet our daily needs, not just our physical needs but also*
> > *when it comes to our need to know You intimately.*
> *Forgive us when we choose to go against Your will,*
> *in the same way that we will forgive those who do evil*
> > *against us.*

*Keep us from being drawn by our personal desires to those
things that hinder Your will from being done.*

When we understand that Jesus was first and foremost
about the business of knowing what God's will was every
moment of the day, the interpretation is clear. And then it's
after sharing this prayer that Jesus imparts the analogy of a
man going to his neighbor's house in the middle of the
night to request bread. Again, unless we understand some
of the cultural context of the analogy, we miss some of the
power of the story. In the beginning of this chapter I retold
the parable from another perspective, adding a few cultural
details to flesh out the viewpoint.

Some argue that this analogy teaches that if we ask for
something of God out of our dire need, He will be inclined
to give it to us out of His great love for His people. While I
agree that from a cultural context that may be true, I'm not
sure I believe that's the ultimate reason why Jesus told the
parable in the way He did.

GIVE US BREAD

It's important to know that in ancient Hebraic culture
bread was considered a staple of life. It was eaten at every
meal. During Passover they ate unleavened bread. The
Book of Exodus records that daily God sent bread to the He-
brews in the form of manna. To go without bread was to go
without life.

Consider also that on several occasions Jesus refers to
knowledge, ultimate truth, and even to himself as bread.
John records in his Gospel an amazing interaction between

Jesus and those who sought Him. During their verbal trans-action Jesus refers to himself and His coming work of sal-vation as the *Bread of Life.*

In the Book of Matthew, Jesus wards off Satan's temptation by quoting the scripture that "man does not live on *bread* alone, but on every word that comes from the mouth of God" (4:4, NIV, emphasis added). It's a comparison between God-given insight and human shortcomings.

I love Mark's account of the Greek woman who begs Jesus to use His power to cast a demon out of her daughter. Speaking in metaphor, Jesus tests the woman's mettle by asking her if He should toss *bread* [His power] intended for the Jews to the dogs. Undaunted, she demonstrates her faith in Him, in His abilities, and His compassion by replying that "even the dogs . . . eat the children's crumbs" (Mark 7:28, NIV).

I don't think it's a coincidence then that in our main scrip-ture of this chapter, the man comes looking for *three loaves of bread.* I am of an opinion that, metaphorically speaking, the bread he seeks is representative of godly knowledge. Three could be a symbol of our triune God. And because we find this analogy on the tail end of Jesus' demonstration of how we should pray, a prayer that undoubtedly is a request for God's will to be known and accomplished, it's a safe bet that Jesus is giving His disciples insight into what God is willing to do for those who'll simply be bold enough to ask for it.

Boldness is a key issue Jesus wants to get through to His followers here. He tells this story of a man who comes look-ing for something in the middle of the night. The man wakes up another family. As it is with our society today, knocking on another person's front door in the middle of the night means it had better be a dire emergency, doubly so back then. Most families lived in one- or two-room houses. The family often laid down next to each other when they slept. A person knocking at the door after the family had retired would likely wake the whole family. But Jesus shares a story where an intruder comes in the middle of the night, unperturbed that he may wake this entire family. Because he has an unexpected guest at his home, he can't afford to take no for an answer. He wants the bread. He must have the bread. The homeowner knows that the man won't go away without it, nor can he afford to let his friend go away empty handed. Culture demands it. So he gives the man what he came for because he's been *bold* enough to come in the middle of the night.

Following the analogy, Jesus challenges the disciples to ask, seek, and knock. For what? For knowledge of God's will in their life, not just for physical things. He promises that if they do that, God will grant them what they seek. It's not a prosperity challenge; it's a "connecting with God" challenge.

And if we read on a little further in the chapter, we see Jesus promises that God will grant us that knowledge by giving us the gift of the Holy Spirit. God's desire is to give us *all* of himself, the greatest gift, the Holy Spirit. Many of you reading this will understand why this is so significant. And in later chapters, we'll talk more about the Holy Spirit's presence in our lives and how critical it is. But for now it is enough to know that this promise Jesus makes is essential to having a gutsy faith.

Jesus gives us a challenge that He wants us to do boldly, with humble confidence, with guts. It's not a challenge that means we are to come to Him with arrogance, but with an understanding that, though we are completely at His mercy, God truly desires to reveal himself to us. We see from this whole interaction that it's not God's desire to deny us that insight, ever. All we have to do is ask for it, with guts, and Jesus promises we *will* receive.

THOUGHT QUESTIONS

■ What insights are brought to light for you when the full context of this whole passage is explained?

■ Review the rewritten version of the Lord's Prayer. Does it give you a deeper insight into what Jesus might have been saying?

■ Have you ever thought of the Lord's Prayer as a prayer for knowing and understanding the will of God and all the aspects that the will of God might encompass?

■ Do you feel you have the right to ask God to reveal His will to you? If not, why?

■ When you pray, do you pray more about personal requests or more for God's will to be revealed to you?

ALL YOU GOTTA DO IS ASK

Scriptural Basis: *Read Matt. 21:18-22.*

 They were all still reeling from yesterday's spectacle. Who would ever have thought that when they entered Jerusalem the people would respond as they did, hailing Him as their King, as their Lord? Who would have guessed the crowds would line the roads with palm branches and cloaks, signifying Jesus' majesty and rule?

Just days earlier, hadn't each of Jesus' disciples assumed their entry into Jerusalem spelled certain doom for their Teacher and for themselves? It was a well-known fact in the region that because of His supposed blasphemy, the chief priests had sworn blood oaths to kill Jesus if He ever returned to Jerusalem. And yet the opposite had actually happened. Rather than receiving a death sentence, the people threw an impromptu parade, as if Jesus were a returning, conquering hero.

And then they all assumed the death knell had tolled when Jesus made an even larger spectacle of himself by turning over all the tables of the Temple-approved merchants and money changers. Jesus accused them of being thieves—murderous talk in most circles. And still nothing happened.

It was as if the whole affair were business as usual for their group. And then, after disrupting the entire Temple economy for the day, Jesus began laying hands on the sick, healing them one after another, as if it were just any other day. Children began shouting out praises to Him, as they often did. The Temple priests questioned His authority to do the things He was doing. And as Jesus often did, He thwarted them by quoting Scripture. Business as usual.

They left Jerusalem and headed for Bethany to spend the night. And now, early in the morning, they were headed back the same way they'd come. Not far off to the side of the road they noticed a fig tree. How odd that it would be in full foliage at this time of year, long after the time when it should have dropped its leaves for the season. A fully leaved tree surely meant fruit could be found on the branches.

Noticing the tree, Jesus paused, contemplating the prospect of fresh figs for breakfast. The disciples, ever vigilant to what their Teacher might do, paused as well, waiting for His lead. Jesus cocked His head toward the tree, indicating His intention, and with a wry smile said, "I could use a snack. How about you guys?"

The procession moved toward the tree, its branches waving in the light morning breeze, beckoning them to come taste the luscious fruit it bore. What a treat! Figs when they were out of season. Reaching the tree, they spread out around it, examining the branches, searching for the fruit that surely had to be present. Nothing. Some of the disciples dug deeper into the barren fig tree's shrubbery. Still nothing.

Jesus stepped back a few paces, eyeing the tree, contemplating. Peter and John watched Him closely. Judas, coming out from under the brush with a look of disappointment on his face, looked to his Master for an answer. From behind the tree they heard Andrew comment, "How can a fig tree be so fully leafed, and yet not have the first fig on it?"

No one else said a word. The wind rustled through the branches. In the distance, birdsong interrupted the awkward silence. In their hearts, as they regarded Jesus in this long, uncomfortable pause, each one knew it was about to be one of those moments, those teaching moments.

Then, not removing His eyes from the tree, Jesus broke the quiet with a simple statement. "May you never bear fruit again!" (Matt. 21:19, NIV). No lightning flashed. No thunder rolled. The wind in the branches did not slow or increase its pace. Nothing indicated at first that something amazing had just happened. The disciples looked at each other, wondering what was supposed to occur, oblivious at first to the almost imperceptible changes in the fig tree.

And then, as if picking up speed, they noticed it. Something was different. The leaves weren't quite as green as they had been seconds ago. They deepened in color, almost black now. And they seemed to be retracting, shriveling, drawing in on themselves. The branches seemed a bit more rigid now, as if they were suddenly old and dry. And now the shriveled husks, that moments earlier were leaves, began to drop from the limbs, some captured by the breeze as it whipped past, some piling on the ground below. The leaves gone now, the limbs continued to contract on themselves until they had curled into a thick knot against the trunk, a massive fist thrust upward from the ground as a last vestige of defiance.

Jesus turned to go back to the road, His hands clasped casually behind His back, leaving the disciples standing there aghast at what they'd just seen. How? Their eyes darted to one another, asking the unspoken, obvious question. How could this be? Finally, one of them dared break the hideous silence. "How did the fig tree wither so quickly?" (v. 20, NIV).

Jesus paused, and turning back to them said, "[It's like this.] If you have faith and do not doubt, not only can you do what was done to the fig tree, but also you can say to this mountain, 'Go, throw yourself into the sea,' and it will be done. If you believe, you will receive whatever you ask for in prayer" (vv. 21-22, NIV).

They watched Jesus return to the road, each frozen in his identical thought, *What's that supposed to mean?*

It's my contention that, like the disciples at that moment in time, over the years the Church has missed what Jesus was saying here. After reading this Bible passage we often are left wondering if Jesus really meant what He said about our faith. We wonder if having faith enough to move a mountain really means that a physical mountain would be moved.

I was recently in my small-group meeting where this topic was brought up. Our small-group leader made the comment that he'd always been taught and had always interpreted this passage to mean that if our faith is strong enough, the "mountains" of our day-to-day trials would be moved. As everyone nodded in agreement, I suddenly blurted out, "Well, why couldn't it be a physical mountain that would be moved?" All the eyes of the group were suddenly upon me, half of them wanting to know what I had to say, the other half wondering if I were just a complete idiot.

Never one to be denied my say, I pressed on. "Do we believe or do we not believe the stories of the physical miracles written in the Old and New Testaments? Didn't God part the sea for the Israelites, or was it just a nice piece of fiction? Did the fig tree actually shrivel up, or was Matthew only recording this incident metaphorically? Why would Jesus have said what He did if He didn't actually mean it? Hasn't God been about the business of working miracles throughout eternity? Or is it just that we, the modern Church, have lost our faith in what God actually can do? And if so, do we justify our lack of faith in His kingdom by suggesting that this passage is speaking only to our daily trials and tribulations? What if God actually asked us to go command a tree to shrivel up or a mountain to be moved? Would we know God's voice well enough to recognize that He was asking us to do that? But even more important than hearing His voice, would we have enough faith to go do what He asked us to do?"

Therefore, if we truly want to understand what Jesus meant in Matt. 21:21-22, we have to look at the context of what was about to happen to Jesus and what had recently taken place before this incident. Remember, much of understanding Scripture is about understanding the context surrounding each passage.

THE END OF THE RACKET

The day before the occurrence in this passage, Jesus had entered Jerusalem in an unprecedented victory parade, a symbolic gesture of the triumphal battle He would soon fight to become our Champion of salvation. His return in such an audacious manner was equally unprecedented, as the chief priests and Jewish leaders had vowed to kill Him if He ever returned to Jerusalem. Everyone knew this, so it was quite an in-your-face move for Jesus to have allowed himself to be lauded in such a daring manner. It was as if He were saying, "Put your money where your mouth is."

Matthew records that Jesus entered the Temple—the very business offices of the enemy, if you will—and overturned all the money changers' tables, tossing out those who were selling sacrificial animals and upsetting the entire Temple financial economy—at least for that day. Why? Why would He do this?

We often point our fingers at selling anything within the church walls as if to say that because of the incident recorded in Matt. 21, Jesus had a problem with selling stuff while at church. The reality is that Jesus did what is recorded here because the chief priests had a racket going. The sacrificial law handed down by Moses had been established for the purpose of allowing God's people to draw close to Him again, to receive forgiveness for their sins, and to sense His presence and love. Yet over the years, the Temple laws had been modified to the point where it became financially impossible for many people to commune with God. People were prohibited from bringing sacrificial animals from their own flocks. "Not clean enough" was the usual excuse. The people were then forced to use those animals purchased from the Temple for sacrificial purposes. Also, only the Temple currency could be used to purchase those animals, a currency that was only good for use within the walls of the Temple. Money changers were notorious for jacking up the exchange rates to increase their profits, a good portion of which were in turn passed on to the Temple priests. So, unless people could afford to have their money exchanged for a pittance, and then purchase their sacrificial animals from the Temple animal sellers—who typically charged more than the standard market value—it was impossible for them to receive forgiveness for their sins or have communion with God.

Another reason for Jesus' reaction was that the money changers set up their business in the Court of Gentiles. The Court of Gentiles was as far as a non-Jew could go into the Temple in order to worship God. Non-Jewish worshipers, while allowed to come this far, were treated with scorn by the Jews, and were often charged even more to exchange their funds for the Temple currency. So the one location where, symbolically, God reached out beyond the Israelites was further being turned into a location of extortion.

There were even more reasons for Jesus' anger. But it is enough to say that this money-changing business was all a racket, a distortion of the Hebrew laws set up to line the pockets of the Jewish leaders. Everyone knew it. And Jesus wasn't going to stand for it. He turned their tables on end and called them thieves to their faces. The Temple leaders were indignant. But little did they know that within a week, events would occur, at their own doing, that would destroy their swindling ways for good. Not only would Jesus be crucified as an eternal sacrifice, once and for all, but also, because of this, the mountainous complexities of the Law would also be tossed out. I just love the symbolism of Jesus' act here. It's as if He were saying, "I'm going to disrupt your plan for at least today. Oh, and guess what, I'm about to take down your whole thieving scheme as well!"

Then the next day, we find Jesus and His disciples standing before a fig tree with all the outward signs that it should have fruit on it, and yet none could be found at all. The fruit and leaf bearing season had passed. For a fig tree to even have leaves on it at any time of year meant it should have fruit on its limbs at some stage of development. Yet the leaves of this particular fig tree were an empty promise, much like the flourishing business being conducted at the Temple. While there was a lot of activity in the Temple, no fruit was being developed. It was time for it to go.

So, Jesus cursed the tree, it shriveled, and the disciples were left wondering what was going on. Then Jesus told them that if they have faith, they can tell a mountain to go drop itself in the sea and it will do so.

Yes. Jesus *is* speaking metaphorically. But we tend to minimize what He was actually saying. Jesus was about to topple a mountain—the dead Church of that day—and the disciples didn't get it. In the Book of John, Jesus makes a parallel reference to this same issue. John 15 records that during the Last Supper, Jesus said that the Father "cuts off every branch . . . that bears no fruit" (v. 2, NIV). Again, a reference to what was about to happen. The Jewish Temple system was not bearing fruit, much like the tree, and Jesus is bidding it farewell, time for it to go. A new Kingdom was about to be established, and nothing would stop that from happening.

NOTHING IS IMPOSSIBLE

So what *is* Jesus telling us through this incident? It's important to understand that since the Fall in the Garden of Eden, God has been about the business of restoring all of creation to himself. In the Exodus, we see God at work, bringing cataclysmic plagues on Egypt, parting the Red Sea, feeding the Israelites with manna, all in the eventual goal of restoring creation. Through the work of the Old Testament prophets, and the work of the judges and kings of Israel, we see God at work restoring all of creation. In the Gospels, we see Jesus performing miracles left and right, all in the interest of restoring creation. God has worked through nature, through the hands of His people, and through His own presence to bring about restoration.

And in Matt. 21:18-22 we find Jesus telling His disciples that if they have *faith* and don't doubt, they can and will move mountains. Jesus isn't just giving them challenging words to deal with their daily trials and sufferings. He's far beyond that. He's thinking of Kingdom issues here. Jesus is challenging them to be so close to God the Father, knowing and understanding His voice so clearly, that when they hear Him whisper, "Go move that mountain," they will know it immediately, and in faith will do so because it will be God's power moving it, not their own, all for the purpose of bringing about restoration.

Remember, we are working from the perspective that Jesus never got a *no* from His Father. Why? Because He never did anything that the Father had not called Him to do in faith in the first place.

On two other separate occasions in Scripture, we find similar situations where Jesus seemingly promises incredible things if we'll just ask for them. In John 14, we find Jesus sharing deep words of wisdom just before He is to be taken away and crucified. During this intimate time we find Jesus pouring out His heart to His disciples, knowing what is on the way and that His time is very limited. We find Him shelling out spiritual nuggets left and right. It's here that He shares one of these miracle-promising tidbits. In John 14:12-14 He says, "I tell you the truth, anyone who has faith in me will do what I have been doing. He will do even greater things than these, because I am going to the Father. And *I will do whatever you ask in my name,* so that the Son may bring glory to the Father. You may ask me *for anything* in my name, and I will do it" (NIV, emphasis added). Anything?

Then in Matt. 17, not long before Jesus' Triumphal Entry into Jerusalem, we find Jesus talking to His disciples after they had difficulty casting a demon out of a possessed child. After asking why they couldn't cast out the demon, Jesus says, "Because you have so little faith. I tell you the truth, if you have faith as small as a mustard seed, you can say to this mountain, 'Move from here to there' and it will move. Nothing will be impossible for you" (vv. 20-21, NIV). Nothing will be impossible?

Three separate occasions and Jesus promises the incredible if we only ask in faith. I find it disturbing that we choose to discount that Jesus might actually mean what He says. Because we have never understood the total context of what He is speaking about, we choose to relegate these promises from Jesus to trivial, convenient matters, as if Jesus were only speaking of our personal sufferings and how we can deal with them. How sad when, truly, Jesus is promising that where God's kingdom is concerned, if a physical mountain stands in the way, and God commands one of His children to move it, it actually will be moved.

I wonder where the Church might actually be today if Christians believed they could move mountains at the asking or cause fruit trees to shrivel at a single command, should God call them to do so. To do so would mean we have guts, real guts.

THOUGHT QUESTIONS

- How have you viewed the idea of moving mountains if we were called by God to command them to do so? Have you viewed this idea as being metaphorical, as if talking only about personal trials? As something else?

- Do you think God still calls His people to command seas to be parted, mountains to be moved, or any other such miracles? Why do you believe the way you do?

- Personally, what mountains or barren fig trees stand in the way of God's will being fulfilled for you in light of His kingdom? What mountains stand in the way of your family? Your church? Your work?

- Identify what fig trees need to shrivel and die before moving forward. Pray about what God wants you to do about them.

WHY COULDN'T WE DO THAT?

Scriptural Basis: *Read Matt. 17:14-21; Mark 9:14-32.*

Their voices could be heard blocks away —anger, resentment, frustration. The volume of each voice slowly increased with each passing salvo of words.

On the ground, outside of the circle of verbal combatants, a man sat cradling a small boy in his arms, desperate hope slipping away from him with the rising cacophony of voices. The boy's eyes were rolled back in their sockets, and save for sporadic body convulsions, he looked as if he were dead or fast moving in that direction.

Then someone in the glut of shouting bodies said, "Look, there's Jesus!" With those simple words the clash halted, if only for a moment, while the crowd looked down the street to where the man was pointing. A short distance away, a broad-shouldered Man stood with three companions, His keen, confident eyes already probing the crowd, wondering what might be going on. A silent heartbeat passed and the throng swept toward Him, shouting, desperate for answers, for anything, for a simple word of greeting from the Master.

Jesus continued to scan the mass of bodies. His disciples were a good portion of the crowd, some of them the most vocal in the group. Amid the shouted greetings and despondent requests, He kept searching the crowd. The mob was an eclectic mix of Hebrew teachers of the Law, common housewives, market vendors, and Roman travelers. Some faces were familiar, some not. Finally, His eyes fell on the man He'd been searching for, the man who had been cradling the child in his arms only moments before.

"'What [were] you arguing with them about?' he asked" (Mark 9:16, NIV), His voice resonant and commanding. At the sound of His voice a hush fell over the crowd.

The frail man pushed his way to the center of the group where Jesus stood. Hope began resurfacing on his face. "Teacher," he began, "I brought you my son, who is possessed by a spirit that has robbed him of speech. Whenever it seizes him, it throws him to the ground" (vv. 17-18, NIV). He motioned to the boy, now a distance away. A woman huddled over him now. Jesus assumed her to be the boy's mother. "[When the spirit] seizes him," the man continued, "it throws [my son] to the ground. He foams at the mouth [and grits his teeth as if he were a mad dog]. I asked your disciples to drive out the spirit, but they could not" (v. 18, NIV).

Jesus looked around the assembly of bodies. Only a few of His disciples were willing to look Him in the eye. Most seemed suddenly distracted after hearing the man admit their failure. Shaking His head, Jesus snorted disappointment. "Unbelieving generation," He muttered half to himself, half aloud, scolding words for those disciples within earshot. "How long am I going to be with you? How many times will I have to show you? How long will I have to put up with your nonsense?" Then turning to the man he said, "Bring Me the boy."

The man ducked away. Moments later the crowd parted and the boy was laid at Jesus' feet. The boy's eyes rolled back into place, only for an instant, and then he released an unearthly shriek and was thrown into uncontrollable convulsions. The swarm instinctively backed away, leaving Jesus and the boy's father standing over the writhing body.

"How long has he been like this?" (v. 21, NIV) Jesus asked as the father knelt to try and control the boy's flailing.

"Since he was very young. I can't count how many times the spirit has tried to kill him," he said. Then looking at Jesus he implored, "If you can do anything, please, help us. We're desperate."

Jesus raised a single eyebrow, as if He couldn't believe that the man was actually serious with his plea. *"If you can'?* [My friend, in case you haven't heard,] *everything* is possible for him who believes" (v. 23, NIV, emphasis added).

"I do believe!" the father replied. "But I need you to help me with my unbelief!" Honesty. Jesus nodded. He could always work with honesty.

On the streets around them a larger crowd was beginning to gather. Not willing to subject this wretched boy and his father to any more spectacle than was necessary, He decided to end this.

"You deaf and dumb spirit. Come out of that boy right now and don't ever return," He stated. The evil spirit in the boy shrieked again in agony, throwing his body in wild spasms of rage. And then the boy fell silent.

"He's dead!" a woman in the assembly of people gasped.

Jesus shook His head, a humorous smile almost cracking His face as His eyes glimmered with hope. Then He reached down, took the boy by the hand, and lifted him to his feet. The crowd went wild as the father wrapped his arms around his son, now whole and free. "Thank You! Thank You!" he could be heard shouting through tears.

Later that night, when Jesus and His disciples gathered together for a quiet moment of reflection, one of them finally broke the tension hanging in the air and asked the question. "Jesus, why couldn't we do what You did?"

"It's simple, really," He replied. "You simply haven't spent enough time in prayer, and so you lack faith. If you have faith as small as a mustard seed, you can move mountains by simply commanding them to move. That is why you struggle. You don't even have that."

— — — — — — —

Let's take a moment to revisit the scripture reference, Matt. 17:14-21. Pulling in the parallel recording of this occasion from the Book of Mark (9:14-32) gives us a more complete rendering of what actually happened.

The first time I read this block of Scripture critically I remember wondering why Jesus seemed so disgusted with His disciples. I mean, He went so far as to call them a "perverse generation" (Matt. 17:17, NIV). I wondered whether it was because of the spectacle they had turned the affair into. Possibly. But that just didn't seem to fit somehow. Was it because He, Peter, James, and John had just spent a life-changing moment on a mountainside, and just after coming down to reality the disciples were immediately confronted by their inability to get the job done? Maybe.

My personal opinion says that had something to do with it. How many times have you come back from a great, spiritually moving event only to have your fond memories quickly dashed against the hard reality of somebody doing something stupid? It happens. And it's really hard to be all smiles and compliments during those times. Remember the story of Moses coming down from Mount Sinai after spending so much time in the very presence of God? After all the Israelites had been through in their journey to this point, after all that God had rescued them from, Moses comes down the mountainside to find that his people had so soon forgotten God, turning instead to a handcrafted statue for their answers. Think he might have experienced some dis-

65

appointment? No doubt about it. However, somehow I don't think that's quite what was going on here.

But investigating what happened around this passage reveals that about a week before this occurred (see Matt. 16:13-20; Mark 8:27-30), Jesus and the disciples were gathered together at Caesarea Philippi for a spiritual retreat of sorts. It was during this time that Peter confessed that he believed Jesus was the Christ, the Son of God. Jesus then conferred on Peter and the disciples the mantle of the Church. He gave them the authority to bind spiritual powers on earth and in heaven.

How disappointing when only a week later Jesus found the very men He had given this authority wallowing in their own incapacities. No, not because they hadn't been given authority. Not because they hadn't seen Jesus effectively demonstrate how to cast out a demon time and again. But simply because they hadn't spent adequate time with the Father in prayer.

WE ARE POWERLESS WHEN . . .

Prayer—the key link to eternity. And those whom Jesus had selected personally couldn't figure out that they were spiritually powerless to do anything God called them to do unless they spent serious time in communion with God, listening to His voice, understanding the work and way of the Father.

Jesus lived His life in full communion with the Father. Every chance He got He escaped the crowds and spent private time with God. His strength and spiritual power flowed from His time spent in prayer. Jesus demonstrated this prayer *necessity* time and again throughout Scripture. Even though Jesus already *was* God—and some might question His need for prayer—He still prayed. And if the Son of God, the One through whom all of creation came into being, carved out regular, intimate time with God the Father, how much more should we do the same?

It's no secret that life is just crazy. We have no clue what the future holds. We find ourselves daily facing mounting problems, conflicts, and turmoil. We fill our spare time with television, movies, friends, sports—the list goes on—all in an effort to escape reality. We will do almost anything to cope with the difficulties we face daily.

My wife and I are acquainted with a woman who is probably the most capable and organized individual we've ever known. She schedules everything, down to the minute. She knows how much time and effort it takes to accomplish even the most menial tasks. As a result she is able to juggle mind-boggling amounts of work, family schedules, personal goals, and church responsibilities. And she possesses an unswerving ability to stay on task. She is the go-to person everyone wants on his or her team because, if she commits to a project, it will get done on time, in budget, and in prime fashion. She's an ace.

The paradox about her is that her personal life is a wreck. Her relationship with her husband is tenuous at best. Her teenage son wants nothing to do with her. For the longest, she's crammed her schedule full of activities, outings, and other business. But even though she schedules everything, she never schedules any time for God. As a result, she never spends time with God. She plays Christianity and can talk the talk. But when it comes to getting vulnerable in front of God one-on-one, she will not do it. Despite all her organizational abilities, she's also made a bevy of bad decisions that have brought her continual disappointment and sadness.

In many ways this woman mirrors our whole North American society. We cram our time chock-full of stuff, yet we can't even seem to carve out 15 minutes a day to pause, to retreat in quiet and prayer with our Heavenly Father who wants nothing more than to empower us daily to face reality.

It's no wonder that on a daily basis we find ourselves in the same situation the disciples found themselves in. Trying to solve our problems—or worse yet, someone else's—without having checked in with God to find out what His solution might be. And then we fail time and again, like the disciples, always wondering why we couldn't get it right.

It's through prayer that we connect with God. It's through connection with God that we gain confidence in His love and care for us. Through time with God we begin to recognize His voice and His imprint on the world around us. We see where He is moving and where He is not. It's through prayer that we ground our faith. And it's through our faith that He can truly begin to work through us.

Some might disagree with me, but I'd go so far as to say that prayer is more important to our faith and spiritual walk than reading Scripture. Now before you brand me a heretic, may I remind you that prayer and faith existed long before the Scriptures did. It's true. Look at the apostle Paul's discourse on the issue in Rom. 4. Without quite saying it, Paul goes around and around about Abraham receiving the promises he did because of his faith in God. When Abraham lived, there was no written Word of God. According to biblical scholars, the first written Word of God didn't come until Moses appeared on the scene. As you know, Moses was a descendant of Abraham's. And yet in Romans, Paul clearly points out that we who are Christians today have that freedom simply because of Abraham's extreme faith in God that came about through his prayer life.

So, history was changed because of the faith and the prayer life of one man, Abraham, who had never once read the first written Word of God. Now you see the basis of my claim. I'm not saying that we shouldn't read Scripture. Far from it. But along with that, we should be spending serious time in prayer.

Which leads us to this impassable truth: without personal prayer in our lives, we will continue to struggle. We want to have the guts, the faith for God to use us to move mountains. But if we don't develop our prayer life, it will never happen.

THOUGHT QUESTIONS

■ Do an honest self-evaluation. How is your prayer life? Strong? Mediocre? Nonexistent?

■ When faced with difficult times, do you bury yourself in activities or do you find time to bring them before God?

- If God were to speak to you during your prayer time, have you spent enough time with Him to recognize when it is His voice? Or would you likely dismiss His voice as a passing thought?

- What changes would you have to make in your life in order to spend at least 15 minutes each day in prayer with God?

- What methods do you utilize to verify what you think God is calling you to do? Search the Scriptures? Share with close friends in Christ? Is it out of character for how God traditionally works?

IN JESUS' NAME . . .

Scriptural Basis: *Read Mark 9:38-41; John 16:23-24.*

7

They were the chosen ones. They were the 12 closest to Jesus. They were the ones the Master sent out to touch, to heal, to cast out demons. No one else should be doing that, especially in the name of Jesus.

So who was this upstart? Who was this man they'd seen driving out demons? And what gave him the right to invoke the name of their Master? He wasn't supposed to do that.

People were coming to him from everywhere because they'd heard he could cast out demons. His reputation was growing. And when they saw him, they recognized him from some past experience, although they could not quite place where. Somewhere they had brushed shoulders with him. Jesus had touched him in some way.

But here he was now, as if he were one of Jesus' personal disciples, performing miracles in Jesus' name. How dare he? He did not have the authority or the right to do that. It had to stop!

John took the lead, approaching the man on their behalf. He explained the way things were. *They* were Jesus' chosen disciples. He was not part of their crowd. *They* had the authority to drive out demons in Jesus' name. He did not. If he wanted to drive out demons, that was his own business. But he wasn't to do it in Jesus' name. *They* owned that copyright, that trademark. The disciples had the corner on that market. And without Jesus' direct permission, he wasn't to continue what he was doing.

The man nodded his agreement to their suggestions. The last thing he wanted to do was cause problems. All he wanted to do was to help out. He didn't want to do anything that was wrong. If helping people in the way that Jesus had helped him was taboo, then he didn't want to break the rules. With some sadness, he dismissed those around him who had gathered requesting his help. Believing their work there was done, the disciples went their way as well, confident that their positions were still secure.

Later that evening, John shared their accomplishment with

Jesus. *No doubt He'll be proud that we protected His reputation, along with ours,* he thought. But much to John's surprise, Jesus wasn't so approving.

Jesus shook His head, disappointment painted across His face. "You guys just don't get it, do you?" He said. "Why would you stop him? You shouldn't have done that." The disciples looked to each other for support, for excuses to justify what they'd done. But by now they'd learned not to argue or to try justifying their actions when He disapproved. Jesus continued. "If he's doing miracles in My name one minute, there's no way in the next he could say anything bad against Me. He couldn't be casting out demons in My name if he was against Me. In fact, anyone who is able to do good deeds in My name, in the name of Christ, will be rewarded."

Jesus continued, but for John the lesson was over. What they did was wrong. They had stopped an ally from doing the work that God had called him to do. In trying to protect their Master's cause, they actually weakened it. He would never let that happen again.

— — — — — — —

Context, once again, is critical. The disciples had just thoroughly disappointed Jesus by not being able to cast the demon out of a young boy, even after they'd been given the authority to do so just a short time earlier. Unsuccessfully they had tried casting out a demon in the name of their Master. Jesus then pointed out that they couldn't do it because they hadn't spent enough time in prayer with the Father.

Then, several nights after that, we find Jesus giving them a lesson in humility. An argument had risen in their ranks about who was the greatest. Jesus responded by placing a child in their midst. In that day children had no influential rank, authority, or societal significance, but Jesus explained to them that they needed to treat even the children as if they were the most important people in the world. It's in the middle of this lesson on humility that John chose to reveal what they'd done.

I'm inclined to believe that John was motivated a bit by guilt. It's likely he realized the disciples had acted out of self-preservation, as if this man were a threat to their position with Jesus. If the man was not in their group and was doing what the disciples couldn't, what would Jesus think?

When we view the Gospels as a whole, we find that this was when John, the disciple who was most intimate with Jesus, wrestled with his own feelings of self-importance. It's shortly after this that we see John and his brother, James, approach Jesus asking for seats of authority when Jesus enters His kingdom. Jesus redressed them with compassion and helped them see that they needed more of a servant's attitude.

But let's get back to the issue here. The disciples shut down a man who was doing what they could not. He cast out demons in the name of Jesus when they were at a loss. And he was *not* a disciple—or was he?

Hadn't Jesus just spent time teaching them that they couldn't cast out demons or work miracles unless they'd spent time in prayer? Jesus had stated that pretty clearly. It doesn't take a degree in deduction to see that the man the disciples had stopped could not be casting out demons if he hadn't spent time in prayer, considerable prayer. No doubt he'd been touched by Jesus in some way or another. No doubt that touch had changed his life—so much so that he finally *got it.* God the Father had given him enlightenment and power. He was working to build the Kingdom, not later, but now. And he wasn't part of the chosen few.

Jesus confirms this fact. The paraphrase of what Jesus said to the disciples goes something like this:

> *Don't stop him! What are you thinking? How could he do a miracle in My name if he wasn't on our team? How could he cast out the legions of the enemy if he was working for the enemy? It doesn't work that way. He's on our side! He's not going to act successfully on our behalf one minute and then turn around the next minute and stab us in the back. He's helping you guys out. Don't you get it? He's helping you guys out in the task I'm about to load you down with. If he so much as gives you a cup of water in My name, I'm going to reward his faithfulness.*

IN JESUS' NAME

Growth is a difficult process. It means sometimes admitting we don't have all the answers. It means realizing that God uses others, who might not be in our inner circle, to teach us lessons about our own shortcomings. Growth requires that we admit that we don't always have the spiritual depth we desire—and that others whom we might learn from just might. It means we have to have our perspective straight. In this case, the disciples had the wrong perspective, but the man casting out demons had his perspective just right. Perspective is often determined by our faith.

I love what Jesus says in John 16. It's down to the final hours of His time with the disciples. He's done just about all He can for them. He is delivering His final words of advice to them. Jesus gives them a fair warning of what *will* happen. And while doing so, He also promises the Holy Spirit to them. In John 16:5-15, Jesus discusses the coming of the Holy Spirit, and what the Spirit will actually do. In verses 13-14, Jesus says: "But when he, the Spirit of truth, comes, he will guide you into all truth. He will not speak on his own; he will speak only what he hears, and he will tell you what is yet to come. He will bring glory to me by taking from what is mine and making it known to you" (NIV).

Then Jesus goes on to inform the disciples that what's going to happen will be very difficult, like a woman giving birth to a child. But once it's all over with, their joy will far outweigh the pain they will feel. Then He says this: "In that day you will no longer ask me anything. I tell you the truth, my Father will give you whatever you ask in my name. Until now you have not asked for anything in my name. Ask and you will receive, and your joy will be complete" (vv. 23-24, NIV).

There are no coincidences where Scripture is concerned. It's not a coincidence that just before Jesus is going to be hauled off and crucified on the Cross that He again comes back to the subject of asking for things in His name, and then promising that they *will* be granted. It's also no coincidence that just before promising this, He lets them know that the Spirit will come and speak to them of things to come.

Does Jesus *really* mean it when He says that anything that is asked in His name will be granted? Remember, this wasn't the only time Jesus promised this in the Bible.

I believe Jesus meant exactly that. Anything asked for in His name will be granted by the Father. The issue at hand is knowing what exactly it means to ask for something in Jesus' name.

In our modern context, we don't really understand what it means to invoke the name of a leader. Our modern, materialistic, hero-driven society has lost its perspective. Name-dropping is a common practice. We use our association with people of authority all the time to get what we want. If we want a good deal on a car we're purchasing, we mention that we know someone in the car dealer's service department who said the front office would cut us a deal. When we want tickets to a sold-out concert, we call our friend who works in some remote fashion with the concert hall, wondering if he or she might have access to any of these elusive tickets. We've associated the use of a person's name with getting what *we* want, rather than getting something on behalf of the person whose name we're about to drop.

What I mean is this. In Jesus' day, a servant would never invoke the name of his or her master unless the master had sent the servant to do his or her bidding. In other words, if the servant were in the marketplace looking for the perfect chicken to cook for dinner, he or she would never say to the vendor, "My master says you need to sell me this chicken so I can cook it for him for dinner," unless of course the master had actually sent him or her to do that very thing.

77

The use of a master's name in coordination with doing something was only done if the master had already endorsed the transaction. To do so otherwise would be to risk possible punishment.

So what's the connection? What connects the man casting out demons to the promise that God will grant what we request in Jesus' name? It's really very simple. The man successfully casting out demons in Jesus' name was doing so because God had already empowered him to do it. He'd spent the necessary time in prayer, seeking God's direction for his life. And when he heard God speak, he did what the Father commanded him to do.

In John 16, Jesus clearly tells the disciples ahead of time that His Spirit is going to come and let them know what they need to do. And then He promises them that when they do what they've been told to do in His name, it *will* be granted because they are doing what God wants them to do, not necessarily what they want to do.

So the issue then becomes understanding what God asks them to do.

THOUGHT QUESTIONS

- Have you ever asked for anything in Jesus' name, believing with all your heart that it would happen, and then didn't receive it? Why do you think that happened?

■ Do you think God was asking you to pray for it, or do you think your request might have been self-motivated?

■ What is the connection between faith and knowing what God is asking you to do in Jesus' name?

SETTING GOD UP TO LOOK LIKE A JERK

Scriptural Basis: *Read 2 Cor. 12.*

No one dared defy him. He was bold. He was confident. He knew his Scripture. He clearly heard and understood the voice of God. He had written countless letters to encourage the Early Church.

In the early days of the Church he had stood as her arch nemesis. Back then he went by the name of Saul of Tarsus. His name alone struck mortal fear into the Early Church. With the authority of the

Jewish leaders backing him, he'd hunted down Christians and had them put to death. Christianity had represented a serious threat to the Jewish faith. Saul was zealous for God. At that point he'd heard of this Jesus and the political string-pulling the chief priests had gone through to get rid of Him and His teaching. Unfortunately, stopping Jesus only seemed to have strengthened His cause. It was that threat that drove Saul to hunt down the early believers under the authority of the Jewish leadership.

And then on one trip to Damascus everything changed. He'd come face-to-face with the Almighty himself. Jesus himself, the risen Lord, had confronted Saul with his sin. Jesus himself had offered forgiveness. Since then, everything was different.

The boldness by which he'd hunted down the first Christians was being used to confront sinners. His eloquence of words and significant biblical knowledge was used to send letters of encouragement to the brothers and sisters of the Way all over the Mediterranean region. What he had once tried to stomp out was now his single focus—the growth of the Church. Now he was known as Paul. Now he operated under the authority of God. His letters of sanction were written on his heart by the Holy Spirit. And he was even more unstoppable now than when he operated under the authority of the chief priests.

But then, there was this issue. He'd kept it private. No one else knew what it was. But he knew, and God knew.

He anguished over it. He longed to be released from it. He'd prayed for God to release him from the burden. And as yet, the answer had always come back no. Instead of removing the burden from Paul's back, God extended grace.

And now Paul had come again asking for release. Prostrate on the floor, weeping in anguish, begging one last time for God to remove his unspoken burden—his "thorn in the flesh."

"God, why?" Paul pleaded. "Why must I go on with this burden? Why do You permit me to suffer, to endure this messenger from Satan? God, can't You see that if I were released how much more I could do for Your kingdom? I'm tormented by guilt. I'm ripped asunder by pain every day. God, please release me. Take away this thorn in my flesh."

And with ever patient peace, the Spirit answered, "No. I'm sorry, Paul. That's not the plan. Instead, I'll extend even more grace to you. You see, that's all you need anyway. Because when you struggle, when you're weak, that's when My power is made perfect. That's when people see Me and My love the most."

Paul never asked for release again. He chose grace instead.

— — — — — — —

At first, all Paul perceived was the pain, agony, and frustration caused by this thorn. He wanted it gone. He couldn't see past it. It was a distraction to him. What he failed to see was that God's plans were much grander. God had plans for that thorn all along.

The thorn's purpose was to keep Paul humble. Second Cor. 11—12 is a series of sarcastic remarks from Paul about all that he really could brag about. But it's during these sarcastic remarks we find out that Paul had something that for a while ate away at his soul. He thought the answer would be for God to remove it. But if God had taken away the thorn, what would be left to keep Paul's ego in check?

We have no clue what Paul's thorn in the flesh was. Honestly, I'm inclined to think Paul's thorn was something big, something that could bring down a man of his stature if the world knew about it. Some inner struggle that likely went against everything he stood for as the very vocal Christian man that he was. But I have no evidence to back that up. It's just my own personal speculation based on God's response to him. God promised him grace. In our context we often use the term "grace" in a variety of ways. We say that God gives us grace to overcome physical ailments, pain, or hardships. And while that's true from the standpoint of one of the definitions we have for the word "grace," it's not the kind of grace God is extending to Paul. This grace God gave him is the kind that is extended to a person when he or she has done something wrong and doesn't deserve to have the wrongdoing forgiven, but it is forgiven anyway.

To me that speaks of some hidden, inner struggle that Paul dealt with on a daily basis. Speculate all you want about what manner of struggle it might be. Give it a name if you like: sexual sin, overindulgence, addiction, hatred. It doesn't matter what you want to label it. The fact is, God gave Paul grace—meaning He chose to overlook the struggle Paul had —rather than take the thorn away from him.

God allowed Paul to live with the thorn, giving Paul the knowledge daily that God still chose him to be the most significant leader in the Early Church. The thorn helped Paul realize he wasn't perfect. It helped him know he would never be able to achieve ultimate forgiveness and communion with God on his own. He had to have God's grace.

It was after the third request that Paul finally realized that he had been asking the wrong question all along. He'd been asking God for something God was never going to give. The first two times Paul asked for the thorn to be taken from him, no doubt he was frustrated, possibly even angry that God wasn't listening to him. But Paul wasn't listening to God at that point. Instead, Paul was setting God up to look like a jerk, as if Paul's struggle didn't mean anything to God.

IT'S ABOUT GOD, NOT YOU

The reality was that the problem was with Paul, not with God. Paul wanted it his way, not God's way. When Paul finally listened, he realized that God's plan was for people to see that even the mighty in faith have struggles. It's through God's extension of grace to Paul that the rest of us can know that when we have struggles, God extends grace to us as well. Knowing that Paul is like the rest of us helps us understand that God isn't looking for perfection. He's looking for humble, contrite hearts.

When people pray and God doesn't answer their prayer in the way they would like, often they get angry with God. They think He is unjust or holding something against them. No matter how noble, morally right, or godly their motives may be, rather than questioning themselves they point the finger at God as if He were at fault. They set God up to look like a jerk instead of searching their heart and Scripture for what God's plan might be.

On the other hand, when our relationship with God is such that we are listening to Him, when we sense the Spirit's voice, then we can begin asking for the right things rather than the wrong things. Does it happen all the time? No. But the more we recognize the voice of the Spirit in our lives, the easier it becomes to always ask the right questions.

And often it takes a lot of guts to ask those right questions.

THOUGHT QUESTIONS

- Does any of this sound familiar to you? Have you ever asked God to remove something from your life that you've struggled with spiritually?

- Did God remove your thorn? Or did He give you grace instead?

- Does it help you with your personal struggle to know that even Paul had personal issues that God wouldn't just make disappear?

- Have you ever questioned whether God was really listening to you when you asked for something, yet He never gave you the answer you wanted?

- During those times, did you ever blame God for anything, as if He were the cause of the problem?

THE RIGHT PERSPECTIVE —THE RIGHT QUESTION

Scriptural Basis: *Read Matt. 26:36-46; Mark 14:32-41; Luke 22:39-46.*

9

The night had fallen. The final Passover meal had been observed. As they made their way through the streets, the night sounds greeted them with each step— crickets singing their night song, muffled voices in the homes, a startled dog barking in the distance, echoing across the valley they had just traversed.

In the voices of the disciples Jesus sensed mixed emotions. A few of them had enough wits about them to know something was going to happen, something big. Others joked with each other, having already put behind them the serious words their Rabbi had spoken moments before they'd left. They did not understand. They were clueless as to what was at stake. Had Jesus come right out and told them that tonight Judas would betray Him and that by this same time tomorrow night He would be dead, they still wouldn't have believed Him.

But then it had to be that way. This was a path that only Jesus could travel. He needed them to be safe. As agonizing as it might be to Him, they had to survive through the weekend so that they would finally understand. If they truly had known what was at stake, they might do something stupid, either getting themselves killed, or worse yet, upsetting the plans that all eternity hinged on.

Finally, they reached the familiar olive grove, Gethsemane. "Let's go in for a minute and rest," one of them suggested. Jesus hesitated. This was the place. He knew it. His final moments of freedom would culminate here. There was a moment of hesitation caught only by John, who searched Jesus' face for answers. Jesus feigned reassurance, smiled, and nodded His agreement.

"Yes, let's go in and rest," He replied and followed the disciples through the gate. As the Eleven spread out on rocks or against trees, Jesus placed His hand on Peter's shoulder. "Why don't you, James, and John accompany Me further into the Garden. I need your presence. The rest of you should remain here."

The disciples were used to this sort of thing by now. Those three were Jesus' inner circle. They didn't give it another thought as the small group moved deeper into the trees.

When they had reached a certain point, Jesus turned to them. "Please, wait here for Me, and pray. I'm . . ." His voice faltered for a moment. "I'm deeply troubled about something. In fact, My soul is so overwhelmed that I feel like I truly could die right now."

James and John exchanged a glance as Jesus moved away. Peter stepped forward, as if to follow, but then stopped, obediently waiting at his Master's request. Jesus moved deeper into the thickening grove, crumbling to the ground finally as the emotional weight of His approaching task overwhelmed Him. From where Peter, James, and John stood they could hear His short, breathy sobs, and they wondered, on this night of Passover, of celebration, what could burden Jesus so deeply?

It would happen soon. There was no denying it now. And Jesus chose to spend His last few moments of peace with His Father, in prayer. The legions of infinity looked on, holding their collective breath as the One through whom all things were created wept in the arms of His Father.

"If it can be any other way, Father, please, let's go that direction!" He sobbed. "But, as always, I want Your will more than anything else."

Then, in the unseen ether surrounding Him, time slows to a crawl, all of heaven's heart breaks over the pain its favorite Son must carry. Unseen masses of angels stand on the precipice of infinity, each one eager to come to the aid of the

Prince of Ages. God the Father cries with His only Son, His pride, His passion. There can be no other way. They have both known it from the beginning. They recall the dance they have enjoyed together from the beginning of creation. They remember the heart-wrenching agony suffered when humanity fell, separating them from their creation by the veil of sin. They recollect the plan of redemption they set into place, the plan that has worked itself out over the eons. And now they both sit on the edge of fulfillment, knowing there can be no other way.

Time collapses on itself—a frozen moment as the Father and Son walk through an eternity of memories, all that they've done to arrive at this point. The victories, the defeats, the conquests, the sorrows—all swirl around them like a miasmic kaleidoscope visible to no other but them. No, there can be no other way. They laugh. They cry. They both know it. They've known it from the beginning. If humanity is ever to understand the depth of their love for it, the absurd lengths to which they would go to restore the covenant, then there was no other alternative.

And from the masses of angels gathered around, a representative is selected to go. He is the hands, the very arms of the Father, sent to encourage and embrace the corporeal manifestation of His Son in these last moments before time resumes its relentless passage.

Strengthened, Jesus stood from where He had been. "I understand," He whispered to the Father. "It's not possible for this to happen any other way. I must drink this bitter cup. I want Your will, not Mine, to always be done."

Time resumed its steady tick. The moment had arrived. At the edge of the garden Jesus could hear the footfalls of the accusers sent by the enemy, making their way to where they were. He could sense it. Taking one last deep breath, Jesus steeled. The deliverance of humanity was at hand.

Bring it on.

▬ ▬ ▬ ▬ ▬ ▬ ▬

While discussing this book with colleagues, I shared my idea that it is never God's desire to say no to us. His desire is always to say yes. They thought I was crazy. *Sometimes God has to say no,* they countered. I agreed with them, but I let them know that's because we are asking the wrong questions. I shared with them the example that Jesus never got a no from the Father. They brought up the Garden of Gethsemane, stating that Jesus asked for the cup to be taken from Him. Jesus got a no then, they said. My counter to that argument was that they needed to go back and reexamine the question He presented to the Father.

A good friend of mine, and one of the most brilliant theologians I know, Jim Hampton, told me once, "So much of what we call 'theology' is based primarily on semantics. Change the semantics and you change the entire meaning of a passage." He's absolutely right, you know. But that idea applies to modern language as well. Where we put the punctuation and where we place the emphasis in our voices can make a world of difference in what is communicated. I would argue, then, that what Jesus asked of the Father makes a world of difference if you understand the semantics.

ONE MOMENT IN TIME

But before we dig into that issue, let's back up and examine what's going on at this particular moment in the salvation story. Some might argue that the most critical moment in the path to humanity's salvation via the Cross was when Jesus' blood was shed and He actually died on the Cross. I would counter that Jesus' last free moments spent with the Father is the most critical incident. All of eternity hinged on what happened at that moment!

Prior to this, there is no recorded account that Jesus ever questioned His purpose or destiny. Nothing was going to keep Him from the Cross. And after this moment, Jesus never looked back. He never stopped and questioned again if another way to free humanity could be found. No. Only once did Jesus even question whether there might be another way, this one time in Gethsemane.

Let's examine what is at stake here. Let's go back to the Levitical laws that the Jews lived by. Understand that God, working through Moses, set up these laws. It was God who established the sacrificial procedures by which His people could attain freedom and forgiveness from their sins. And it was through this sacrificial system that they could attain peace with their Maker. It was through the shedding of innocent blood that their sins were forgiven. It was a vicious, brutal system. But then, dealing with sin is always an ugly affair.

Fortunately for us, from the very beginning the system was flawed. God set it up that way. The system was flawed in that the shedding of an innocent lamb's blood was not enough. It had to be done again and again, year after year, in order to keep the people cleansed from sins. It was not easy. It took a lot of work that came at a price, the loss of innocence.

God set it up that way to show humanity they could never achieve redemption on their own. No, there had to be a perfect sacrifice to seal the deal once and for all. If humanity was ever to move on, if humanity was ever to understand the depths of God's love for them, if humanity was ever to know the lengths and depths He would go to redeem them from the hell they had created, God would have to become flesh and become that sacrifice. He made the rules. He would live by them, until by the shedding of His own blood, He broke their power. The answer was determined from the very beginning. There *was* no other way.

So, if there was no other alternative, why would Jesus even raise the question? Let's examine for a moment what Jesus is facing. Jesus knew what kind of death He was about to suffer. It would be brutal torture. I don't know if any of us could imagine the physical agony He was about to undergo. I'm not sure Jesus really did either. But I doubt the threat of physical pain was what drove Him to ask if there was another alternative. Pain *could* be endured. Pain is temporary. For One who viewed reality from an infinite perspective, the time He spent on the Cross writhing in pain might hardly register.

But although He understood the scope of infinity, He also had never spent one microsecond in all of eternity out of the presence of His Heavenly Father. Jesus knew He was headed to the Cross to be the ultimate Sacrifice for us. Doing so meant one thing: humanity's sins, for all eternity, would be heaped on Him at His death, and He would experience what it would be like to be separated from the Father as He finally understood the loneliness of the sinner.

One way of looking at this would be to compare Jesus to a man who willingly chooses to be drowned for the sake of some great purpose. He enters the water knowing what to expect—he is going to be plunged under water until his body no longer has life in it. If he stays above water, his body will get the air it desperately needs to stay alive. Knowing that, he still goes under the water willingly. People above the water line grip his body to ensure he stays under. He holds his breath. Time ticks by. His body begins to crave air. But he knows he will not get any. He wants air; his brain tells him he must have it. He fights the urge to struggle, knowing if he doesn't drown, the great purpose will not be achieved. Air! He must have air. He has willingly separated himself from it, but he needs it. If he could get just one breath of air, he'd be willing to go back down and try the drowning thing again. Would the hands securing him allow him just one breath, one more small breath of air? Coherent thought begins to break down. Eventually he can no longer control his autonomic functions. His body breaths in, but there is no air available, just water, and by now his mind has gone as well. Very shortly after that, his body functions shut down due to oxygen deprivation to the brain, and he is gone.

The analogy isn't the best, but hopefully you have a closer understanding. The body's desire for air is strong. But for One who has never known the depravity of sin—whose very existence has been the antithesis of sin for all of eternity—His repulsion to what was coming and His desire to never have to experience sin outshines our desire for air in the same way the sun outshines a flashlight. There really is no comparison, but it will give you a vague idea. To willingly accept the Cross, knowing it meant He would literally take on all of our sins, took every fiber in Jesus' being. So, you can understand His hesitation at this point.

THE REAL QUESTION IS . . .

Let's get back to where we started this chapter. Did Jesus receive a no from the Father when He asked if the cup could be removed from Him? If you think Jesus' question really ends at that point, the answer is yes.

But I don't agree that His request ended right there. No, the key lies in the petition Jesus actually made. I love how Luke phrases it best. In Luke 22:42 Jesus states, "Father, if you are willing, take this cup from me; yet not my will, but *yours* be done" (NIV, emphasis added). It's a loaded statement, but it's the right one. My paraphrase of what He asked goes something like this: "God, you know, for all of eternity, I've never experienced a moment of sin. If there's any other way we can bring redemption to humanity, let's do it. But more than I want my way, I want to do what You want Me to do." As always, Jesus asked the right question. His perspective is always right. His perspective is God's perspective. And He gets what He asks for: God's will to be done, or rather, the salvation for all creation.

Obviously, Christians aren't God incarnate as Jesus was. It's impossible to always see things from God's perspective. But adjusting the attitude and the approach of the question makes a world of difference.

Many people finish their prayers with statements like "Your will be done, Lord." But do they truly mean it? Is it just habit or are they honestly seeking God's will in their prayers? If they are, why do they fret so much when circumstances don't turn out as they wanted them to? If they are trusting God fully, should it matter?

Asking the right question comes first from being in touch with God. But even when we may not hear the voice of the Spirit clearly, we can still ask the right questions, assuming we can truly accept what God's will is for us, even when it differs from what we want. It may be semantics, but it is so significant. Acceptance of God's will for us is critical, and it takes guts.

Sometimes, God's will may mean placing ourselves in harm's way. It may mean risking everything. It usually means we will be out of our comfort zone. But that's precisely when faith takes guts.

THOUGHT QUESTIONS

- Have you ever asked for something in prayer and ended the prayer with "Your will be done"? Did you *really* mean that when you prayed for it?

- If you have ever prayed for God's will to be done regarding any particular situation, and then it didn't turn out as you had hoped it would, were you disappointed that God did not grant your prayer as you thought it should be granted? If so, why?

- Have you ever prayed something earnestly, not knowing what God's will was in the situation? Describe a situation that fits those circumstances.

- What would you like God to do in this situation? How will you feel if it does not turn out that way?

- Would it be better to ask God to reveal His will first, and then ask for the right thing after you hear from God? Why or why not?

SEEKING THE HEART OF GOD

Scriptural Basis: *Read Luke 11:1-4.*

Jesus had gone to do what He always did, pray. He'd gone to meet with His Father. Those meetings were His strength, His fortress. His prayer life was everything to Him. During them He prayed not only for himself but also as an example for His disciples.

He knew that by now His disciples were beyond suspecting He was more than just another rabbi. Now they truly were beginning to believe He might just be the Messiah their people had anticipated for so long. The trip to Caesarea Philippi and the events since then were convincing them more of that fact each day. So it was important for them to know that the Son of God spent time daily praying, connecting with His Heavenly Father.

As Jesus wrapped up His prayer time in His quiet place, He noticed one of His disciples watching Him. Jesus smiled, happy He'd been caught in the act. His disciple nodded in return, but his face remained solemn. Questions, curiosity, knit across his furrowed brow. Jesus knew the question the man pondered before he even asked it. But he waited for it, happy to allow the disciple his own time to formulate what was on his mind.

"Lord, John taught his disciples how to pray. Teach me— teach us—to pray as You do."

It had finally happened. The disciples wanted to know the secret. They wanted to know how to touch the Father's heart. He knew that they thought it was something complicated. But Jesus was happy to show them just how simple prayer actually was.

"All right," He responded. "Here's what you do when you pray . . ."

—— —— —— —— —— —— ——

In chapter 4 we discussed Luke's version of the Lord's Prayer. But for the sake of refreshing our minds, let's recap. Only this time, I'll add in the extras we often include when reciting the Lord's Prayer corporately. Understand that many current translations of the Bible leave these additional portions out of the text.

For background knowledge, these parts are left out because the earliest copies of the New Testament manuscripts in the original Greek do not include them. Some believe these were added into later manuscripts because they were included in Matthew's version of the Gospel. Of course Matthew's accounting of the Gospel differs from Luke's also in that Jesus taught this prayer during a different phase of His ministry. Without going too far down a bunny trail, some scholars believe that because Matthew's version teaches this prayer at a time different from Luke's, the Bible is in conflict with itself. I'm inclined to believe that because prayer was such a critical part of who Jesus was, there's a high probability that Jesus taught the disciples how to pray more than once. I'm also guessing Jesus taught them the same format each time. Hence the differing accounts. But regardless, because saying them has become a part of our tradition, and because these words appear in Matthew's Gospel, let's use them here for emphasis' sake.

> *"[Our] Father [in heaven],*
> *hallowed be your name,*
> *your kingdom come.*
> *[May your will be done on earth as it is in heaven.]*
> *Give us each day our daily bread.*
> *Forgive us our sins,*
>> *for we also forgive everyone who sins against us.*
> *And lead us not into temptation[, but deliver us from the*
> *evil one]"* (Luke 11:2-4, NIV).

Matthew's rendition has Jesus teaching how to pray as a part of the Sermon on the Mount. There, Jesus clearly says that personal prayer should be a private event between a person and God. Prayer isn't done as a show of piety or verbal eloquence. In fact, Jesus almost goes so far as to say it's not how many words a person uses or what kind of show is put on. Jesus' example of prayer is very short and to the point.

Again, for emphasis as I did in chapter 4, and so you may receive a clearer understanding of what Jesus is saying, here's my paraphrase of the Lord's Prayer:

> *Father,*
> *You're holy, and everything associated with Your name is holy.*
> *May everything that builds Your kingdom happen as You see fit.*
> *Just as it's always done in heaven, may Your desire for our lives always be fulfilled here on earth.*
> *Meet our daily needs, not just our physical needs but also when it comes to our need to know You intimately. [Fill in what requests you have here, but keep them short and sweet.]*
> *Forgive us when we choose to go against Your will,*
> *in the same way that we shall forgive those who do evil against us.*
> *Keep us from being drawn by our personal desires to those things that hinder Your will from being done.*
> *And keep Satan off our backs.*

That's it. Pretty simple. Short.

MUCH MORE THAN TALKING

So, if the prayer Jesus taught His disciples to pray was so short, how could He spend so much time in prayer? If that's all we are to pray, why should it take up so much time?

For some reason, we often have the mistaken idea that prayer should be filled with our talking to God. I've got a sneaking suspicion what Jesus fails to mention is that a great portion of His prayer life was filled with silence. That's right, silence.

As we discussed in chapter 4, God is really OK with us coming to Him—with guts—and boldly bringing our requests to Him. But what is far more critical is that we finally shut up and listen—shut our mouths, shut our brains off, and just listen.

How many times in the Old Testament do we find God coming to the patriarchs of the faith during their times of silence? Need some examples? Moses, alone on the mountain. Samuel, alone at night in his bed. David, as a shepherd out in the fields. Elijah, alone in the cave. Daniel, alone in his room.

When Jesus prayed, we often find Him going to "a lonely place" by himself. In the Garden of Gethsemane, He took three companions, but only so far. He still separated himself. He got alone. What does He instruct us to do before beginning our prayer? That we should go into our prayer closet and shut the door.

Being alone with God is key. Silence. Solitude. God wants us to put away all the distractions and listen to Him. He wants to come to us, filling us with His presence, soothing our wounded hearts, cheering our tumultuous minds, reviving our broken dreams. The same One who spoke the universe into existence wants to speak with you as well. But too often we won't be quiet long enough to hear Him, to sense Him moving.

I'm convinced the reason why the Church in the United States and Canada is statistically declining is because our media-driven, materialistic world has gotten increasingly noisy. We have lost the ability to be silent. Everywhere we go there is music, commercials, media, newspapers. We have been so swayed by a profit-driven, results-minded, selfish society that to be still, to do nothing but listen, means we are wasting our time. We have begun to fear silence. People fall asleep with their radios going, or their televisions running, simply because they fear the silence.

It's this lack of silence that prevents us from hearing the voice of God. It's because of our impatience that we miss His direction.

Silence takes guts! It is contrary to what we have been brainwashed to believe. But without it, we will continue to be ineffective. Without it, our faith will falter. Without effective prayer—including significant amounts of silence—we will have no faith and our Christianity is fruitless. How will we ever get to the place where we are always asking the right questions if we never allow God His time to tell us what we need to be asking for?

We can't. That's why we get the *no* answer so often. Or why the answers to our prayers are often delayed. That's why when God doesn't answer our prayers as we hoped He would, our spiritual walk is in turmoil. We never stop to listen.

THOUGHT QUESTIONS

■ How much time have you spent in prayer lately?

■ How much of that prayer time was spent bringing requests to God, and how much time was spent in silence, listening to God?

■ Is it difficult for you to be silent in your prayer time? If so, why do you think so?

■ Did you hear God speak to you when you prayed? If not, why do you think you didn't?

THE HEART AND SOUL OF IT

Scriptural Basis: *Read Mark 12:28-34.*

11

This rabbi was different. This teacher of the Law truly sought the heart of God. He had studied the Scriptures diligently. He did not see God as vengeful. He understood the compassion inherent in the Law, the protective, omnipotent blanket woven throughout the Torah. Often he found himself at odds with his fellow teachers. He had grown used to it after so many years.

But then he heard of a new Rabbi who seemed to have the heart of the people. This Rabbi's reputation had grown over the last two years. Most of the priests in the synagogues spoke ill of Him, however. All the better, he reasoned. He had hopes of meeting Him one day. It would be good to have the ear of someone else whom the rest of their crowd disagreed with.

And then, as luck would have it, when he had made the pilgrimage to Jerusalem to observe the Passover with his own disciples, this other Rabbi—this Jesus—happened to be in the city as well. He had to meet Him. He'd heard that there was a rather sizable cavalcade over the previous weekend when Jesus arrived in town. He'd chuckled when he heard that the chief priests were furious about the incident. *Good for Jesus. It's about time someone else shook things up around here,* he thought.

Today he'd taken his students to the Temple to listen to the other teachers share opinions of the Law. It always made for great discussion later in the evenings. When they'd arrived, Jesus was there. Rumor had it that the Pharisees and Sadducees had been at Him all day, trying to trip Him up, hoping to locate a flaw in His proverbial armor, seeking to discredit Him.

When they arrived, there was a great crowd gathered around Jesus, most of them rabbis and their students. He pressed his way through the crowd, eager to meet the Man himself, uncaring if he left his own students behind, indifferent to offending anyone by his unyielding push to the front of the crowd. He had to meet the Man.

He listened closely to Jesus' voice as he pressed through. His ability to speak was unfaltering, commanding, authoritative. This Man *knew* the Law, as if He might have had a hand in writing it. But that thought seemed silly to him. Still . . .

By the time he arrived at the inner circle, Jesus was wrapping up this particular debate—a bunch of heretical Sadducees trying to trip Him up on issues of resurrection, which they did not believe in anyway. Idiots!

This Jesus was not what he had expected to see. He dressed like a commoner, an everyday workman, unlike the finely robed teachers he was accustomed to dealing with. Besides His clothing, He had every appearance of a working man as well—broad shouldered, rugged faced. His hands were thick, sturdy, and showed signs of callusing as if they had spent years in a workshop or something of the like. Where had this Jesus come from? Certainly not the normal crowds he was accustomed to dealing with.

"He is not the God of the dead, but the living. You are badly mistaken!" Jesus was saying. The Sadducees Jesus was reproaching, anger written on their faces, wanted to bring a counterattack, but having been so soundly thwarted, they hesitated. After exchanging dubious glances with each other, it seemed better to leave well enough alone. Yes, the teacher liked this Jesus.

As the Sadducees skulked back into the crowd, he could not resist. He had to get Jesus' opinion. He went straight to the issue. "Of all the commandments, which is the most important?" (Mark 12:28, NIV).

Jesus turned and regarded him. Jesus' eyes, His piercing eyes, looked right through the teacher, to the core of his being. The rabbi almost drew back, at first wanting to hide, as if his entire life were suddenly exposed. But then an approving smile crested Jesus' lips. He knew, the teacher was sure Jesus knew somehow, that he truly wanted to hear what Jesus had to say. He was positive Jesus knew he wasn't there to test Him as all the others had.

"[Here's] the most important one," [Jesus answered.] "'Hear, O Israel, the Lord our God, the Lord is one. Love the Lord your God with all your heart and with all your soul and with all your mind and with all your strength.' The second is this: 'Love your neighbor as yourself.' There is no commandment greater than these" (vv. 29-31, NIV).

The teacher was shocked. He didn't know why, but he was. It was what he had been teaching for so long. To hear someone else in agreement with him was exhilarating. He looked around him. As luck would have it, several of his staunchest opponents were looking on and were within earshot. He raised his voice so as to be sure he would be heard.

"Well said, teacher," he replied staring Jesus in the eye. "You are right when You say that God is one and there is no other but Him. Loving Him with all that a person is—his whole heart, his complete knowledge, and his entire strength, and loving your neighbor as yourself—these are more important than all the burnt offerings and sacrifices we could ever bring" (see vv. 32-33).

Jesus nodded approval at him. Staring him straight in the

eye, unblinking and serious, He said, "You are not far from the kingdom of God" (v. 34, NIV).

—————————

It's not enough for us just to hear God speaking to us and then to ask the right questions. More important than that is to love God, really love Him. So the question then becomes, do you love God? Do you? Have you really asked yourself that question? Have you done a self-examination to find out where He stands on your love meter?

It's sad to admit, but many people walking through the doors of our churches on a weekly basis don't love God. They're just fulfilling some sort of commitment they feel burdened to perform each week. They go to church out of obligation instead of out of their love for a Heavenly Creator.

When we truly understand the lengths and depths God put himself through to win our salvation, it's difficult not to love. If you've never seen Mel Gibson's *The Passion of the Christ*, you should. In it Gibson depicts the vicious brutality God subjected himself to at the hands of His own creation, offering himself up willingly, playing by the rules He established, all for the sake of demonstrating just how much He loved us and wanted freedom for us! Yes, all because of love for us.

Unfortunately, our society generally has a fairy-tale idea in our minds, painted by countless Hollywood movies depicting love as a temporary emotion existing for the purpose of giving us a rosy feeling all the time. While it's true we will have those rosy feelings at times, it's not a true depiction of what love really is.

Love is commitment. Love is sticking around even when the rosy feelings disappear. Love doesn't give up just when everything turns for the worst. Love doesn't run away from reality, it faces it head on, with guts. Love doesn't give up. It keeps on keeping on! Love is hard, and on occasion, the fairy-tale idea of what love is crops up and makes it all worth it.

Is that how you feel about God? Would you give up everything just to be with Him? According to Jesus, you can keep all the rules of the Bible that you want. You can pray all you want. You can sacrifice all you have. You can do good deeds until you're completely tapped out. But if you don't love God—with *everything* that you are—you have missed the point of it all.

NUMBER TWO IS . . .

Jesus goes on to say that the second most important thing we can do for the Kingdom is to love our neighbors as ourselves. How much do you love yourself? Come on. Be honest.

Some of us have differing levels of self-love. Because of significantly negative experiences in our formative years, some of us have pretty low opinions of ourselves, as if we don't deserve to be loved or cared for. These unfortunate situations have a way of working themselves out in very destructive ways. So why don't we rephrase what Jesus said this way: "Love your neighbor in the way that you desire to be loved."

Is that how you treat those you work with, your neighbors, those you come in contact with? I'd venture that for the most part, your answer is no. Our society, our friends, the media—all have fed us a steady diet of "What's in it for me?" The old saying "You are what you eat!" has equally as much weight where our mental diet is concerned. Self-adulation has a firm grip on our culture, and it's not loosening it's fingers anytime soon.

Think about it. When making a decision with or about another person, when was the last time you thought, *What would be better for him?* If the decision didn't involve a family member or best friend, did that even come to mind?

Jesus says that this is *the* second most important command. It isn't easy to do. And there are no quick fixes. It takes a lot of guts, sometimes, to put others before our own self-interests. But loving our neighbors requires that.

It's a critical issue if our relationship with God is to be shaped the right way. And if that is what we want, then we don't even have to ask if it's God's will for us. Trust me. If Jesus said it, there's no need to have a debate in prayer about it. If loving God with all of our being and loving our neighbors as we love ourselves is not where we are at spiritually, the primary prayer we should have when we present our requests to Him should be that God will change our hearts to match up with what He's said in His Word. And we should mean it when we pray it. Yes, that kind of prayer takes guts.

THOUGHT QUESTIONS

- What kind of love do you have for God? Passionate? When it's convenient? Out of obligation? You don't know?

■ What about your love for your neighbors? Who do you view as your neighbor? Who do you think God views as your neighbor?

■ Does it scare you to have to ask God to change your love for Him and for your neighbors so that it matches up to His will? Why or why not?

■ What are you willing to give up in order to find that kind of love?

IT'S
ALL
GOOD

Scriptural Basis: *Read Rom. 8.*

She held herself, arms wrapped tight across her chest, a pair of brown high-healed pumps dangling from her bruised left hand as she trudged blindly down the avenue. By now she'd lost all feeling in her bare feet as they plodded through the debris-covered streets, the nylons that had formerly encased them now nothing more than threadbare tatters. The enormity of the smoldering, tragic war zone far above the streets of

New York had not completely sunk in on her. All she knew was that somehow, miraculously, she had escaped.

Sarah's mind raced back through the chain of events that had brought her to this place. The concussion resulting from the explosion as the plane ripped into the side of the tower where she worked had thrown her up against the wall of file cabinets she'd been standing in front of, knocking her senseless momentarily. She vaguely remembered hands lifting her from the carpet and rushing her to the stairs. Sarah still had no idea how many floors above theirs the bewildering event had occurred, but it had to have been close. And until they'd descended a few flights on the jammed emergency stairwells and someone had received a call from a loved one on their cell phone, no one really knew exactly what had happened.

Several times as they painstakingly descended from the heights, their downward progress came to a complete halt. The tension and anxiety in the air as they'd all waited impatiently in the tight, claustrophobia-inspiring confines threatened to choke her. Even now that she was out and moving away from the buildings as swiftly as she could, remembering the desperate, panic-stricken descent still clawed at her sanity.

The mind-numbing miasma of screeching sirens, flashing emergency vehicles, and shouting rescue workers overwhelmed her. Ashes, paper, dust, and small bits of debris swirled down the breezy streets and around the masses of people slowly plodding away from the World Trade Center buildings, down the maze of streets, alleys, and walkways, anywhere that led away from the twin towering infernos.

Sarah's mind could not focus. The dizzying swirl of noise pressed in on her from every direction. She wanted to scream. She wanted to weep. Only one question kept running through her head. *Why, God? Why?* But there was no answer. Just the clatter of voices, sirens, and emergency radios.

Nothing registered until she heard a shocked voice shout, "Oh, my God! It's coming down!" Sarah followed the gaze of the horrified woman. And then she, too, froze momentarily, allowing the surreal situation to register. Where the black smoke had been rolling out of the side of the building, a growing blur of gray matter mushroomed out and downward. And then the noise registered, a rumbling, tumultuous thunder, like the sound of one long explosion, unceasing, growing in intensity. And with it the screams and terror of the people around her in the streets. And suddenly, Sarah was aware of the press of people rushing past her, away from the disaster.

Run!

And she did. She did not care where. She did not think. All she could do was turn and flee. Frantic, terrified, it barely entered her mind that she was being pelted by smaller pieces of debris as they reigned down from the heights of the doomed building. The ground below her feet shook. The air whipped past her, heavy with concrete dust, pushed away from the base of the dying building as it crumbled in on itself. It became increasingly difficult to navigate the crowded streets as each passing, reckless moment, the streets filled with the thick, gray cloud.

Sarah could not breathe. She could not see. And then she went down, having tripped over something large and solid. She barely managed to get her arms out in front of her before she hit the cold, hard pavement.

She lay there unmoving, aware that the thunderous blast of the collapsing structure had ended, but the shouts and screams of desperate people rolled on. Her head pounded, not necessarily from physical injury, but from the knowledge of what had just happened. The building was gone. Undoubtedly, people were dead, hundreds or more possibly.

How could something like this happen?

"Why, God?" she choked. She sobbed. "Why would You let this happen?"

— — — — — — — —

If you haven't read Rom. 8, you need to right now. The points raised by the apostle Paul in Rom. 8 are deep, and you'll need to have read it in order to track with where we're going.

Life is hard! It *is* now, and it *was* in biblical days. The Early Church was under persecution. Paul knew that all too well as he was one of the primary figures who had ushered in the persecution of the Church.

How, then, could Paul have the audacity to make these statements in Rom. 8? In verse 28, how could he say, "In all things God works for the good of those who love him"? Especially given that Paul's life, above all, had been no picnic. Over the course of his Christian life he'd been beaten, stoned, and left for dead; had various other life-threats; been jailed, shipwrecked—the list goes on. At his own hands, before becoming a Christian, no doubt he could testify of numerous Christians who had paid the price of their own lives simply for being a member of *the Way.* Acts 7 details Stephen's death as just one example. So how could jail or the loss of one's life fall under the category of working "for the good of those who love him"?

What about today? In the aftermath of the 9/11 tragedies? When war rages in the Middle East, as it has for decades now? When devastating natural disasters like the 2004 tsunami leave hundreds of thousands dead, homeless, widowed, and orphaned? How could a statement like that possibly apply today? How can we believe that *all* things work to the good of those who love God?

As the most glaring example in recent years, in the case of the 9/11 World Trade Center attacks, how many Christians' lives have been irreversibly changed by that tragic event? What happened that day was evil, pure and simple. Since then I have heard well-meaning individuals try to justify what happened by misquoting Paul's statement here. They usually say something like, "Everything happens for a purpose," or "God must have had a reason for this to have allowed something so tragic to happen." Ever heard anyone say something like that? How about yourself? Have you ever made a similar statement?

I'm sorry, but I cannot subscribe to that particular view of

God. To make such a declaration, or even to believe that God had anything to do with 9/11, means we are ascribing evil to a holy God. That would mean everything we have been taught regarding the holiness of God, about His love, about His purity in Spirit, is all wrong.

On the other hand, it does beg the question of how God could allow such evil events to occur. Why does evil of such magnitude happen in this world? And how can anything good come from it?

UNDERSTANDING THE INFINITE

Deep questions. But before venturing an answer, allow me a little leeway, a little grace, in order to delve just a little into the ideas of infinity. Stay with me just for a moment. I'll bring it back to the point.

You may find it humorous that, educationally speaking, I am a rocket scientist. That's right. I hold a master's level of education in orbital mechanics and space technology. Yep! The same skill set associated with the joke "well, it doesn't take a rocket scientist!" And please don't ask the obvious question. I have no idea how a person goes from being a rocket scientist to my current ministry position other than to say it was a God thing.

Nonetheless, let me draw from my educational background in physics to offer some menial explanation to the possibilities of how it may work. Drawing from several theories, scientists believe that from *any* given occurrence in history—meaning anything from scratching a person's head, to coughing, to extremes such as killing an individual, or you name it—there are an infinite number of possible out-comes. These infinite outcomes are each an occurrence in history, which also has an infinite number of outcomes. In short, we exist in an infinite time-stream of infinite events, resulting in infinite possibilities.

God, who exists outside of the flow of time, sees all these infinite possibilities, at all moments in time, all at once. Is it possible that God, in His infinite wisdom, intervenes at times, or chooses not to intervene at times, because the alternative in infinity would be infinitely worse? It's not an answer, it's just a postulation. But this idea helps us later with some possible conclusions about how God can work all things to the good of those who love Him.

Regarding Hebraic culture, many understand that it is based upon the Law God established in His written Word, specifically the first five books of the Old Testament, known as Torah to Jews. Torah is the written tradition of conduct and worship. But besides the written Word of God, Hebraic culture is also based upon an oral tradition that has been passed down from generation to generation since before Torah came into existence. That's right. According to Hebrew rabbis, the oral tradition they have passed down rabbi to rabbi predates the written word.

In the *Handbook of Jewish Thought,* Rabbi Aryeh Kaplan shows how the Hebraic oral tradition of teaching concurs with the above assumptions about God and infinity. Kaplan states:

> God is spoken of as being "eternal," that is, as existing outside the realm of time. Time as such does not apply

to God Himself, only to His creation. God therefore has neither beginning, end or age, since these concepts would imply existence within a framework of time.

God Himself is therefore absolutely unchangeable and unchanging. He thus said, "I am God, I do not change" (Malachi 3:6, NIV).

As Creator of time, God can make use of it without becoming involved in it. He can therefore cause change in the world without being changed Himself. God is thus called the "unmoved Mover."[1]

I think we all would agree that according to Scripture, God is infinite and omnipotent, and that nothing occurs outside of His *permissive* will. "Permissive" being the operative word there, meaning He doesn't cause evil things to happen, but often He allows them to.

Exactly how, then, can we reconcile wicked, tragic, and devastating events with a loving God? Al Truesdale's book *If God Is God, Then Why?* attempts to bring some answers to this very question. Set in the shadow of the 1995 bombing of the Alfred P. Murrah Federal Building in Oklahoma City, the characters debate classic theories on how God could let such a tragic event happen and why evil exists at all in this world.

The closest the characters come to actually finding an answer occurs when they discuss the "free will defense." In it the characters make the following assertion:

Real freedom to choose the good and all that is excellent necessarily includes real freedom to choose evil and all that is degenerative. The possibility of choosing great values necessarily includes freedom to choose disvalue.

A world where the absence of evil is assured will also be one where worship of God and moral excellence are absent. C. S. Lewis commented that if we exclude the possibility of suffering and evil from finite freedom, we succeed only in excluding human life itself.

To speak of creatures who have freedom to choose the good, but who do not have freedom to choose evil, is nonsense. When God created humankind, He set in motion magnificent possibilities for exercising human freedom. But in so doing, He also set in motion the possibility that humankind would badly miss the divine vocation.

Those who think that the reality of evil presents a major obstacle to confidence in an all-loving and all-powerful God should examine themselves, not God. They are the ones with the problem—a problem of elementary reasoning.[2]

For a moment, put aside the idea that God exists outside of time, or that He sees all infinity as one, and if He did not, the above definition for why evil happens falls through. For it to be true, it would mean that God set the world into motion, and then chose not to interfere, allowing nature to always take its course. However, we know that not to be the case. Throughout the Bible and all of history, God's people can point to clear occasions where God did intervene.

One character in Truesdale's book makes the following

statement that seems to sum up the issue: "Even if God doesn't eliminate all evil, given the fact that He is all-powerful and all-loving, doesn't He have a responsibility to nip in the bud major disasters such as the Oklahoma City catastrophe? Couldn't He have caused Hitler to have a fatal heart attack in 1931? Who would have ever charged Him with acting arbitrarily?"[3]

In the end, Truesdale's characters can find no explanation for why God would allow such tragic events to happen. Our earlier hypothesis about God working outside of infinity does not help either. That's because, if there are infinite possibilities, there are an equal number of alternatives, or tragedies, each of which it appears that God could opt for. However, it does lend a measure of assurance to know that God does, on occasion, and according to His purposes, intervene on behalf of His people, and just possibly because He sees that the infinite alternatives are exponentially worse.

In the end, no one has been able to fully explain the mysteries of why evil exists or why God would allow it to continue to exist. The Bible offers no reasons for why God allows tragic events to happen and at other times appears to avert tragedy. The Book of Ecclesiastes confirms that.

HEALING THE PAINS

Fortunately, the Bible does offer answers to the spiritual and emotional pain we suffer from such tragic events. While the answer to the question of why evil exists will likely never be answered, the God of Eternity gives us an answer for the pain evil brings by giving us the Cross. When tragedy strikes, God is there with us, weeping with us in the pain of loss, in the agony of recovery. The Cross sums up all suffering, all humiliation. When God could have easily chosen to forgive humanity by changing the rules, instead He chose to abide by the rules, suffer for us, to understand all pain, all death, and all devastation. Imagine the loss and separation He felt by heaping on His own Son the infinite sins that His own creation brought on itself.

So when a mother laments the loss of a child due to calamity, God is there with her, arms around her, lamenting in her pain as well. When a nation is crushed by natural disaster, God is crushed as well. When a father's heart breaks at the pain his child suffers from the ravages of cancer, God's heart breaks too. He is not an aloof and uncaring God. He is a God who willingly chose to suffer with His own creation. He is a God who daily suffers with each of us when misfortune strikes.

Therefore, because He chooses to suffer with us, He also chooses to bring about a brighter tomorrow whenever He can to those who love Him. The resurrection of Christ is in itself a declaration of God's power to overcome even the most destitute situations. While our theory of how God sees infinity might not provide an answer for why evil exists, it may provide some insight into how God can bring about good from tragedy. If He truly does see all time as an infinite stream of possibilities, He can move tragedy into triumph within that stream. For those willing to cleave to God during those times, for those who have the guts to allow God to heal them, He chooses to bring good.

I'm reminded of God's words to Paul in 2 Cor. 12:9, "My grace is sufficient for you, for my power is made perfect in weakness" (NIV). God is looking for those with the guts to allow Him to move in during tragic times, to bring healing to pain and suffering, to bring love to the unloved, to bring justice to the maligned. He is searching for those who, during their times of weakness, will turn to Him, allowing Him to show His incredible compassion for their situation. God is looking for those who will choose to allow Him to prove just how powerful He actually is. He's desperately seeking those who will free Him to display His perfected power during their times of weakness.

THOUGHT QUESTIONS

- Have there been painful times when you have questioned why God would allow such tragic events to happen? How did you deal with them?

- Have you ever blamed God for tragedy? Why?

- How did you reconcile your blaming God? Or have you reconciled the issue? Do you still blame God? Why?

■ During your personal times of pain, who have you turned to for strength and healing? Family? Friends? Other? God?

■ If you have blamed God for your tragedy, have you ever considered that it might have been caused by the enemy of your soul rather than God? If not, why haven't you?

HE HEARD THE VOICE

Scriptural Basis: *Read 1 Sam. 3.*

13

It was all Samuel had ever known. From his earliest days, all he ever recalled was life in the Tabernacle. He knew his parents, loved them dearly. But he viewed them more like close relatives rather than father and mother. They were the ones who came to visit on a regular basis. They weren't with him every day, training him, educating him, feeding him, or guiding him. His mother had given him to God's service before he was even born, and it was in the Tabernacle that he had been raised.

Eli, the high priest, was more like a father to him. Though Samuel was truly a servant in the Tabernacle, Eli treated him more like a son. And though Eli was advanced in his age, and had failed miserably with his own children, he was a good surrogate father to young Samuel, teaching him all he knew regarding the Law and life within the walls of the Tabernacle. Most suspected Eli secretly hoped that he could somehow start over with this young one. Under Eli's tutelage, and as Samuel grew, the two had become very close.

This night had been no different from the rest. All had retired for the evening. Eli was in his usual bedchamber resting soundly, while Samuel lay on his sleeping mat in the outer chamber of the holy of holies, the place where the ark of the covenant was stored. Samuel lay there unmoving, staring at the darkened ceiling, watching the reflected light from the lamp in the Tabernacle dance its chaotic gyrations across the blank canvas. It was so silent he could hear the slow, steady rhythm of every breath Eli drew in his distant room.

He thought back over hushed conversations he'd overheard between Eli and some of the other priests. As the high priest, only Eli could go into the holy of holies, into the actual presence of God, to bring the requests, the petitions of the people. It was during these times that God revealed to the high priest the direction Israel was to take. Yet in recent times, God revealed less and less to Eli. The other priests were worried, and they questioned Eli increasingly as to the meaning of why God was becoming silent. Eli had no answer.

"Samuel," a distant voice called, interrupting the boy's thoughts.

"I'm here," he answered, springing from his sleeping mat and rushing to Eli's chamber. "Here I am," he said. "You called?"

Eli jumped reflexively, startled from his deep slumber. "Huh? What's that?" a heartbeat passed as he put his thoughts together, realizing the boy had mistakenly assumed he'd summoned him. "No. No, I didn't call you, son," he grunted. "Go back and lie down."

Samuel nodded, confused by the old man's reaction. *Maybe Eli had been talking in his sleep,* he thought as he returned to his mat. He lay down and closed his eyes. The silence returned as quickly as he settled in.

"Samuel!" The boy sat up quickly. He had heard his name again, clearly. It did not sound quite like Eli's voice, but who else could it be? He and Eli were the only ones here. Samuel rushed to the old man's bedchamber once again.

"Eli, I've come. You called me again."

Eli raised up on one elbow, his bushy, gray eyebrows and full beard in disarray from the night's attempted slumber. "My son," he said to Samuel, "I did not call you. You are hearing things. Go back and lie down."

Confused, Samuel turned to go back. Behind him he heard Eli moving around in his bed, trying to find a comfortable position. "Must be having a bad dream," he heard the old man mumble to himself. *I'm not dreaming,* Samuel thought. *I haven't even fallen asleep. Someone has been calling me.*

Samuel had just settled himself when he heard the voice calling him. "Samuel!" Ever obedient, but a bit perturbed this time, Samuel rushed to Eli's room.

"Master Eli, I've come again. You called me." Eli propped himself up on his elbow again, this time staring the boy in the face, his brow knit together in contemplation. Samuel felt the old man's eyes examining him, no doubt wondering if he might be inventing these "callings" for amusement. In the dim light, Samuel could not tell if his master was angry, frustrated, or too tired to collect his thoughts. It was a long, uncomfortable silence. Then Eli's expression softened and one eyebrow raised, as if realization of some sort had come over him.

"[Samuel,] go and lie down and if he calls you, say, 'Speak, LORD, for your servant is listening'" (v. 9, NIV).

Returning to his mat one more time, Samuel made himself comfortable. He breathed in deeply and closed his eyes. The night silence returned, so much now that in addition to Eli's deep, restful breathing he could now even hear the flickering flame of the lamp as it cast its eerie shadows on the unremarkable ceiling.

And then suddenly everything seemed different. He felt a warmth, a presence, right there in the room with him. Someone was there. He opened his eyes and looked around. He saw no one, but there was no mistaking it.

Someone was in the room with him. But for some odd reason, Samuel wasn't afraid. The presence he felt seemed welcoming, as if he had been there all along.

And then he heard the voice, the same voice he'd heard every other time. But this time it was different. The voice was like a field of lilies opening simultaneously in the bright light of a cool spring morning. Like water suddenly flowing from a well, presenting itself to a parched and thirsty desert traveler. Like eternity had been opened up and he were seeing a glimpse of it for the first time. And he did not fear it.

"Samuel! Samuel!" It was as if he had been waiting his whole life for that voice to call his name. He knew the voice.

"Speak, for your servant is listening," he called out (v. 10, NIV).

And at that moment, Samuel knew his life would never be the same again.

━ ━ ━ ━ ━ ━ ━

Let's examine for a moment the manner by which God communicated to the people of Israel before the Crucifixion. When God wanted to communicate to the people, He did it primarily in two ways: through a prophet or through the high priest.

God chose a prophet because of his or her devotion to Him. Usually, prophets had a special skill or unique way about them. But always, their devotion to God and His sovereignty was unquestionable.

On the other hand, and despite their lofty position in Jewish society, the high priests were not always men of God. They were chosen more for their status in Jewish society and less for their devotion to God. But because of their position, they were the only ones allowed to stand in God's presence, behind the veil of the holy of holies. The ark of the covenant, the oracle where God met and spoke to His people, was kept behind the veil of the holy of holies. It was the job of the high priest to stand in the presence of God, to serve as God's mediator to the people of Israel, and to bring to God the special petitions of the people. It was through the high priest that God generally directed the nation of Israel.

However, there were times when the high priest did not do such a great job of relating God's will for the Israelites. Usually it was a case of either sin entering the life of the high priest or his becoming corrupt. In Eli's case, while he personally had not committed any heinous sins, his sons had. And because Eli would not publicly depose his retched sons, he became unusable to God. Instead, God chose to find another mediator for Israel, Samuel, Eli's apprentice, a young boy hungry for the things of God.

When reading the Old Testament, the Bible details how God spoke clearly to the prophets and the high priests. And it was through these prophets and high priests that God handed down His will for the Israelites. And God was usually very clear and specific about what He wanted them to do. It has always been His desire for His people to know exactly what He wanted them to do. He does not like things to be in question.

The New Testament records that at the moment of Jesus' death on the Cross, the veil in the Temple that only the high priest could go behind, the veil that literally protected all of humanity from standing in the deadly, physical presence of God, was torn in two from the top to the bottom by unseen hands.

Why? What's the significance? Why would this veil be torn open? Because at Jesus' death, God put an end to the physical barrier that had been erected to protect the world from the holiness of God. The shed blood of Christ ended the need for humanity to work through a mediator in order to communicate with God. The torn veil opened what was once held sacred and secret to a world that had limited access to God.

It's important to understand that from the point of view of the Jews in that day, the holy of holies was the visible dwelling place of the Spirit of God. We understand now that Jesus was the actual visible dwelling of God on earth at that time. However, when the veil was torn in two, things changed. The Spirit took up residence in the home Jesus spoke of so eloquently in the Book of John. The new temple, the new holy of holies, became the hearts of those who would willingly choose to accept Jesus as their Lord and Savior.

Let's spell this out so we're clear. The Christian heart is the new dwelling place of the Spirit of God. It is within us—the new temple—that God chooses to make His home. Since the fall of humanity in the Garden of Eden, God has been working to rebuild and reconnect in a special and personal way with His creation. He does that by taking up residence in the hearts of His people.

WHY WE DON'T HEAR

So, if God has changed His mailing address such that now He lives in our hearts, and if it is truly God's desire for His people to know His will, why is it such a difficult thing to actually know what His will is for our lives? I mean, if God can choose a boy like Samuel—who didn't have the privilege of having God actually living within his heart—to communicate his message to His people, why are we, whose hearts are the new holy of holies, so doubtful that we could know what God might have in store for us?

I believe that if we say we do not hear God's voice directing our steps in His way, one of several issues must be at hand:

1. Sin is resident in our lives. Unrepentant sin will always shut off communication with God (remember Eli?).

2. We have not spent time in prayer, in meditation, quieting our hearts so that we can hear the voice of God.

3. We have heard the voice of God in our lives, do not like what His voice says, or we don't trust that what we heard was actually God's voice, and so we choose to ignore it.

4. We have our own agenda we would like to see happen, so we choose not to listen to God when He speaks. In other words, we keep asking for what is outside of the will of God.

When we spend purposeful time in prayer, when we spend

silent time listening, truly listening to God, then hearing God's voice really isn't the difficult part. He speaks loudly. Sometimes it's as if He's shouting at us.

No, hearing God's voice really isn't a problem. That's right. I don't believe it's such a difficult thing to actually know what God's desire is where our participation in His plan is concerned. It's the "obediently following God's will" point where the problems come in. Throughout history, God has purposefully made His will known. When He reveals that will to His people, He never capitulates. He doesn't change His mind. He doesn't waffle. To say God changes His story would be contrary to the nature of who He is. If we believe that God is all-knowing, and knows our future, then it would be illogical to say that He would tell us to do one thing, only to waffle later and change His mind. God doesn't operate that way. He knows what He wants His people to do. He calls them to obey.

After hearing God's voice, it's where we move back into the world that requires guts! Society has issues—a lot of them! Most of them stem from a self-centered ideology that we've been fed from an early age. We want our way. We want what's easiest and what we perceive as being most beneficial for us. Generally, doing God's will in our lives doesn't involve benefiting us on a personal level.

Also, doing God's will often seems to put us out of our comfort zones. For a self-centered society, that doesn't sit well. Our society possesses great problems of low self-confidence. We think, *I could never do something like that.*

But what we fail to see is that all God is looking for is availability and willingness. We don't have to work out the details. It's God's responsibility to deal with that. We only have to be willing. Don't believe me? Check out the Bible.

Did the apostles grow the Early Church? No, God did. All the apostles did was preach the Word when they had the chance. God did the rest.

Did Moses have to free the Israelites? No, God did. All Moses did was convey the messages God called him to deliver.

Did young Samuel have to lead the nation of Israel? No. All he did was say, "Speak, Lord, your servant is listening." And then Samuel shared whatever message God told him to.

Truly, if we had to work out the details and make God's will happen on our own, it wouldn't be a God thing, would it? If we had to pull all the strings, it would be us doing all the work, not God. In such a case, why would we even need God if we had the ability to accomplish the impossible?

So if all we have to do is say, "Speak, Lord, your servant is listening," and then simply obey, knowing God will work out the details on our behalf, why do we have such a hard time obeying?

Because hearing God's voice and then obeying what He calls us to takes guts!

THOUGHT QUESTIONS

■ Have you ever experienced hearing the voice of God? What did His voice sound like?

- If you have never heard the voice of God, or if you experience times of silence, why do you think that is the case?

- Have you ever felt God calling you to do something and not followed through on that call? Why?

TOO TIRED TO DEAL WITH IT

Scriptural Basis: *Read 1 Kings 19.*

14 The victory had been complete. No one could have doubted the power of God after what had happened on Mount Carmel. True to form, God accomplished the impossible, obliterating the water-soaked sacrifice, the wood, even the stones of the altar. And God did His work in such remarkable fashion that the people rose up against the prophets of Baal and tore them to shreds.

But then had come the murderous threats of Jezebel. And despite his belief in the power and protection of God Almighty, and even in the face of undeniable victory, Elijah ran. Perhaps because he knew the atrocities Jezebel was capable of, or perhaps out of shear exhaustion, fear gripped his soul like fangs imbedded in helpless prey. So, Elijah bolted for safety.

Onward he trudged, day in and day out, desperately putting as much distance between himself and the she-devil who had enraptured King Ahab and who had entranced the nation of Israel, turning them all away from the one true God. Finally, a month and a half later he collapsed in the mouth of a cave, high on the side of Mount Horeb.

Why me, God? he wondered as he sunk into restless sleep.

"Elijah?" Like a sweet melody heard from a distance above the whisper of a refreshing, spring breeze, the Voice called to him, coaxing him from oblivion. For the longest time Elijah lay there, enjoying the presence of the Voice, enraptured by the infinite possibilities it seemed to offer. He knew the Voice oh too well. He loved the Voice. It was his constant companion. Finally, Elijah gave in to his conscious mind.

"Elijah," the Voice said, "what are you doing here?"

"God, I've done all You've asked me to. You know my passion for what You ask me to do is fanatical. But Israel has forgotten all that You've called them to do. They've abandoned Your laws and killed all Your faithful servants. I'm the only one left, and now they want to kill me too." Even as he rattled off his excuse, the memory of the victory at Mount Carmel traipsed through his mind. He quickly pushed the thought aside, as if that would hide the truth.

With endearing patience beyond description the Voice replied, "Go out of the mouth of the cave and wait for Me. I'm about to pass by."

Elijah knew not to question. He went to the mouth of the cave, hiding just inside. In the distance he heard the rush of wind as it whipped through the valley, growing in strength and volume in its approach. And then suddenly it was upon him, like a vicious snare ambushing unsuspecting quarry. He gripped the surface of the cave wall, desperately holding on for his life. A tremendous vacuum tore at his body. Hurricane-force winds whipped through the air as the funnel of a vast tornado swept across the mountainside. Despite his hiding place, debris, sand, and rock tore at his skin. He reached out with his soul, wondering if God's presence might be the cause of the wind. But he sensed nothing. God wasn't in the tornado.

The wind died slowly and Elijah eased his handhold on the mouth of the cave, but only for a moment. As he waited, the ground beneath his feet began to vibrate ever so softly. The vibration increased in intensity, rumbling, shaking. The cacophony was deafening. Elijah dug his fingers deeper into the crevasses of the cave wall and again reached out, seeking the presence of the Lord. But the violence was empty, devoid of anything godly.

As the reverberation eased, so did the tension in his fingers. But then he felt the temperature rising rapidly. Wildfire swept up the mountainside, eating up what sparse vegetation clung to the sides of the mountain. Elijah pulled back a short distance, protecting himself from the intense heat. As with the previous two disasters, his heart revealed that God was not in the fire.

After the wildfire swept past the mouth of the cave, Elijah wondered what might be next. The stench of charred wood and burnt undergrowth choked him. And then he heard a gentle breeze blowing. It swept across the mountain, rattling the blackened twigs and undergrowth, banishing the foul stench clinging to the air, promising life again to the dead hillside.

And Elijah knew that God was near. He stepped outside the mouth of the cave, eager to meet the Almighty, to bask in His presence, to breathe in the breath of creation.

— — — — — — —

It really doesn't matter what the rest of that story unfolds. Most people plod on about the lessons Elijah learned when God spoke to him on the side of the mountain. Others like to focus on the reasoning of why Elijah ran in the first place. In my opinion, people who focus on anything else but what happens when Elijah walks out of the mouth of the cave have missed the entire point of this biblical account.

True, God did have something to say to Elijah. Something along the lines of, "Are you nuts? Have you so quickly forgotten what I did to the altar and sacrifice on the mountaintop a few weeks ago? And guess what? You're *not* the only one in the world who's serving Me, pal." Sarcasm aside, God did have important issues to discuss with Elijah.

But for me, the point I can't get away from in this story is *when* Elijah knew to walk out of the cave. Let's recap. Elijah was exhausted from his desperate 40-day trek-for-life away from Jezebel. Alone, dirty, and no doubt delirious in the maw of a desolate cave, God seeks him. Elijah's cry for God to end his suffering is strangely familiar. It's the same cry most of us have lamented to God when life reaches its lowest point. And in his desperate moment, God invites Elijah to come outside for a glimpse of eternity. Elijah claws his way to the mouth of the cave and waits for God to pass by.

I don't know about you, but if I were in Elijah's shoes, and God told me to come out to see Him, I'm pretty sure when the wind started ripping the mountain apart I would have assumed that was Almighty God doing His thing, and I would have jumped out of the mouth of the cave, no doubt to my own doom. Or when the ground shook and the fires scorched the earth, I would have popped out of the rocky orifice only to meet my demise head-on. We expect an Almighty God to do those kinds of things, right? I mean, He's God, right? Booming voice, mountains crumbling before His greatness, and all that.

But not Elijah. He waited. Even in his delirious state of mind, he was so attuned to the presence and voice of God that even though God is quite capable of appearing in the mighty wind, the devastating earthquake, or the unquenchable fire, Elijah knew God hadn't arrived on the scene. He waited patiently, safe inside the mouth of the cave as nature tore itself apart outside.

Then when the cool, calming breeze arrived, Elijah's heart quickened and he held his breath. God had arrived. The old, familiar, eternal presence he longed for had descended from the halls of heaven to commune with Elijah. He knew God was near. There was no mistaking it. Elijah stepped out of his hiding place into the welcoming heart of his God.

In reality, had most of us been in Elijah's place, as soon as something extraordinary happened we'd have assumed it was God and exited our domain of safety only to meet our immediate end. The reason is because God often works in ways contrary to what we expect Him to. We expect Him to make His will known to us with flashes of lightning and thunder. We want the spectacular. We anticipate incredible "Ah ha!" moments of deep revelation and grandeur. And yet, more often than not, God simply speaks in simple, ordinary ways.

His Spirit speaks to our hearts, our minds, our conscience, with dialogue that transcends the audible word. More often than not, His presence is found in the calm whisper of gentle breezes.

HOW DO WE *KNOW* IT'S GOD'S VOICE?

It's a valid question. How do we *know* it's the voice of God speaking to our hearts? How can we be sure we're hearing God and not ourselves, or worse yet, the enemy?

It might be easier to answer this question by pointing out that there are certain things God will *never* call us to do. Really? *Never?* That's right, never. What I mean is that God will never call His people to do something that is contrary to His nature, His personality, or His written Word, the Bible. No matter how clear we think we might be hearing God's voice, if it contradicts who God is and His written Word, it's a sure bet it's not God's will.

A few years ago one of my dearest friends, Susie Shellenberger, wrote a book titled *Stuff You Don't Have to Pray About.* Though it's a relatively small book, and it's written with a teen audience in mind, it's got to be one of my favorite books ever. The premise is that, as the title implies, there are certain things that you just don't have to pray about to find out if God is calling you to do them. Susie has a knack for getting right to the heart of the matter in her writings. During the introduction she says the following:

> How could I say I knew what God wanted me to do without having to ask Him? Because God's Word makes it clear that He has given us spiritual gifts that we are to use for Him (see Romans 12:6-8). I know God has given me the spiritual gift of teaching. So, when asked if I would teach a class of adults and disciple a small group of teens, I already knew what God wanted me to do. I didn't need to ask Him about the decision. He had already made His will clear by revealing to me the specific areas in which He had gifted me.
>
> You see, there are some things we just don't need to bathe in prayer. Why? Because God has already settled several issues in His Word. To continue going over the same old ground only prevents spiritual growth.[4]

How true that is. How often do we pray for something, and then when God provides the opportunity, we continue praying about it, wondering if it's the *right* opportunity? In such situations, I fully believe that God lets us know ahead of time what He wants us to do. In our inner heart He places a longing to fulfill His will. And if we have spent time praying for the opportunity to arise, our hearts truly let us know when the right opportunity comes. There is a peace that comes along. It's as if we were drawn to it. And if we've trained ourselves to listen to Him, we *know*.

It's usually our insecurities, both in ourselves and our relationships with God, that prevent us from jumping on the chances when they avail themselves. We hear Him calling us, opening the doors of opportunity, and we worry whether we are capable of doing what's been asked. We lack the guts in ourselves to follow through. We don't have to go on praying about it; we just have to obey.

The other extreme is when we choose to be so blind to Scripture that we ask for what blatantly contradicts God's written Word. Rest assured, God will never call you to do something that contradicts His written Word. For many, that statement may seem like common sense. But there will be some who read this book who are struggling with what they might think God is calling them to do, even though they know it contradicts the very nature of God. An example might be a married man thinking God might be calling him to leave his wife and family for another woman. Or a financially strapped woman with access to the business payroll account, believing God might be telling her to borrow some of the business funds, on a temporary basis of course. Rest assured, if you are feeling moved to do something along these lines, it isn't from God. Do the right thing. Stop asking God if it's His will. Just don't do it. Trust me. God will *never* ask you to do something contrary to His written Word.

WHEN IT SEEMS LIKE IT'S OK . . .

What about those times when what we feel God is calling us to do *isn't* contrary to His Word, His nature, or His personality? How can we be sure it's God calling us to do it?

Again, referring to Elijah's account, even in his exhausted state, even though he was seeing reality through a weary, dim fog, he was so familiar with the voice and presence of God that he knew exactly when God showed up. There was no question when to go out of the cave. God's very presence moved him.

We, too, often find ourselves in a mental state similar to that of Elijah. We each run across times in our lives when we are so exhausted by life itself, so out of touch with what God has been doing around us, that we are capable of irrational behavior, much like Elijah experienced. Despite the godly victory Elijah had just experienced on Mount Carmel, he immediately forgot the power God wields, and he fled when the face of evil threatened him. And it wasn't as if he hadn't received death threats from Jezebel in the past. I've often wondered if Elijah had held out for just a little while longer, could he have been the instrument by which God struck down Jezebel too? Who can say? But it is interesting to think about.

It's easy to point fingers at Elijah, but the real question is, have you ever been there? Life is drowning you. You've just come through incredible times, and suddenly things aren't going so great. God is working all around you and you can't see or hear Him at all. So you run. God is throwing open the doors for miracles each day, and you hide in distant caves, crying out for it to just end.

Fear. Insecurities. Pain. They all blind us to God working in our lives. And maybe during those times, we are running from the very thing God is driving us to do.

And yet, even in the middle of such circumstances, God speaks to us. It's during these tenuous times that we have a few strategies for discerning the voice of God in our lives. Not all of us are prophets, as Elijah was, completely familiar with God's presence. Therefore, I can recommend several policies we need to adopt to make discernment easier during these times of living hell.

■ Follow the Word

Again, back to the excerpt from Susie Shellenberger's book, there are certain issues that God makes perfectly clear in His Word. We should turn to it daily but especially during times of exhaustion and turmoil. It's difficult to make a wrong move when we are steeped in the Scriptures. God speaks very clearly through the Bible. That should be stop No. 1 in godly discernment.

■ Historical Interpretation of Scripture

Beyond just knowing what God's Word says, it's also important to understand how the Church has interpreted Scripture throughout history. God has traditionally spoken to the

Body of Christ in clear ways. Therefore, we need to ensure our interpretations of what we feel God is saying to us align with the Church's historical take. It would be unlikely that God would call a believer to move contrary to how He's been moving the Body of Believers across time.

■ Logical Rationale

Some people might balk at the idea of using a logical review process as a means by which we determine if God is calling us to do something. However, when we review the process of all creation and God's movement throughout history, we see He always moved in a logical, reasonable manner. God never has operated in a random manner. Likewise, in preparing a person for a calling, God also operates in a logical manner. God equips and prepares His children for the dream He has for them. He doesn't randomly call people to perform acts they aren't outfitted to accomplish. He moves us, with meticulous care and logic, to where He needs us.

Therefore, if God moves us rationally, it is wise to consider our calling in light of how we have been equipped. It would be absurd to think God would call one who is tone deaf into the area of music ministry. If we are gifted in or passionate about a particular area we feel called to, it stands to reason that God would call us to that area of ministry.

■ Experiential Understanding

Assuming we have been gifted in a particular way, and assuming we believe God equips the Body of Christ by moving individuals through training, as it were, preparing each for a place within the Body of Believers, then it follows that one's experiences serve as a training ground to better the Christian community. God doesn't generally call people to one assignment and just leave them there. He desires to continually move us to bigger and better things. God is always about the business of growing the Kingdom. By example, refer to the parable of the talents. The servant whom we consider evil was the one who chose not to exercise his ability, choosing instead to sit stagnant. He was punished for not trying to move ahead with what he'd been given. Why? His decision was self-serving and inwardly focused. He was afraid of losing what he had, not concerned about gaining more for his master.

When we look at the whole picture, we realize that our personal ministry and life experiences often serve as a road map for our ultimate calling. Using our past experiences as a benchmark for whether it is God's voice we are hearing can be an excellent tool for discernment.

Along with that, the collective experiences of others within the Body of Christ can serve as a benchmark by which we compare what we hear God calling us to. Experience brings understanding. The collective experience of the Body of Christ over the years has brought a wealth of understanding. Sharing what we believe God is saying to us with those who are spiritually more mature can lend an assurance that cannot be achieved otherwise. For that reason we can and should rely on the experiential understanding of the Body.

THOUGHT QUESTIONS

- Have you ever found yourself, like Elijah, in such a desperate situation that you ran instead of trusting God to take care of the details? Describe the situation and what happened.

- How do you know when God has arrived on the scene and is talking to you?

- When you feel God might be calling you to something, what process do you use to determine if it is God calling you or otherwise?

- Have you ever acted on what you thought was God calling you to do something, only to find out it wasn't God after all? Describe the situation and what the outcome was. What clues did you have along the way that it might not have been God?

- Are you reluctant to respond to God's call? Why do you think that is? What insecurities do you have that keep you from acting with more guts in your spiritual walk?

PUREST DELIGHT

Scriptural Basis: *Read Ps. 37:4.*

The lingering twilight of dusk lit the outside balcony with a haunting nostalgia, drawing him like a parched horse drawn to water. Aided by his servant, David edged to the balcony overlooking the city, his city. At the edge he gazed out at the houses surrounding the palace and breathed deep the temperate air of sundown. The air was saturated with the smells he had encountered countless times, but never quite like this. Succulent roasting lamb from the kitchens far below in the palace.

The spicy aroma of common life on the streets far below. The dank scent of livestock droppings mixed with the sweetness of fresh hay from the royal stables.

It was as if he were experiencing them all for the first time in his life, rather than what would likely be the last time. He wondered if others went through similar experiences when their lives were at an end. Yes, death was near for David. He knew it. He could feel it. And he was at perfect peace with it. God, his God, was calling him home. His son Solomon now sat securely on the throne. There was nothing to fear.

He breathed deep again, focusing on the stench rising from the stables. The sheep, the beasts of burden—they took him back to his days of youth. For a moment he was back in the wilderness, tending the sheep of his father, Jesse. Staff in hand, wind in his wild, matted hair, he watched the sheep grazing lazily on the sparse vegetation of the rocky terrain. David lingered in the fond memory, wishing he could go back to those days, anxious again for the pure, simple delight he used to find in being in the open wilds, communing with God, wrapped in the very presence of the Spirit. But then, in a short time, he really *would* be in the presence of God.

David smiled to himself, thankful for those early days he'd spent in the wilds. It was there he learned the secret of life, the secret of everything. It was there he discovered that to delight oneself in God *was* life. Nothing else mattered.

His love for God was the source of his strength. His passion for God had fueled his creativity. His desire for God's presence drove his leadership abilities. God was everything to him.

Over the years he had occasionally lost sight of that reality. It was then that he struggled. With reluctance he recalled the deplorable incident that had brought about his marriage to Bathsheba. Though he loved his wife, he still struggled with the circumstances that had brought about their union. Back then, war and arrogance had taken him to a place where he regularly forgot to seek God daily. As such he'd orchestrated events to bring Bathsheba, then the wife of another man, into his bedchamber. And then later, he even arranged for that man's death when David's improprieties caused Bathsheba to become pregnant. He had been stupid, so stupid.

But even then, when the depths of his depravity brought him to his knees in utter repentance, God's grace brought complete forgiveness. And even though that one act of rebellion opened wide the gates of turmoil and unrest for his family since then, David had rediscovered the joy of God's presence and the pure soul-delight God's Spirit brought with it.

The horizon was now dark and imperceptible in the distance. Stars in the night sky seemed pinholes in the dark blanket overhead, faint glimpses of the eternity that awaited him. He breathed deep once again, this time far less aware of the aroma of the city. This time all he sensed was God's presence.

Patting gently the hand of the servant supporting him, he looked out over the city once more—the dozing, silent city.

It was time to go. David scuffled back toward the balcony doorway. Time to say his good-byes. Time for the end to come. He smiled again. God was near, very near.

━━ ━━ ━━ ━━ ━━ ━━ ━━

I'm inclined to think that the Church has got it all wrong. And we've had it all wrong for quite some time. For the longest time we've been taught to bring our requests, our concerns, our pleas before God, and lay them at His feet. Then we trust that God will answer our prayers.

Don't misunderstand me. I'm not claiming that this practice is incorrect. Instead, I'm wondering if maybe the number of requests we need to bring before God could be lessened if first we took a different tack. The reality is, when we approach our relationship with God in that manner, it's a pretty self-centered approach. The "bringing our requests to God" approach is more about us than it is about God.

Something about what David wrote in Ps. 37 smacks of his viewing a relationship with God in a completely different way. His whole approach to God was that his responsibility was simply to *delight* in God's presence and let God deal with the matters of life.

I think that's what Jesus was trying to impart to the people in Matt. 22 when the Pharisee, in verse 35, tried testing Jesus. Love God first, above all, was Jesus' response to what was the greatest commandment. In chapter 11 I used the Gospel of Mark's account of this interaction as a larger illustration. Matthew treats this account slightly differently, but the premise remains the same. My abbreviated interpretation of what went on there goes something like this:

"Jesus," the Pharisee's expert in the Law inquired, "what do you say the most important commandment is?"

Jesus, intrigued by the man's approach at testing Him, responded without hesitation. "'Love God passionately, with all that you are. With all your heart, with all your mind, and with all your soul. With everything that you are.' Nothing is more important than that command. And the next greatest commandment, which is almost as important as this one, 'Love your neighbor as you love yourself.' Everything revolves around these two commands. Do these and everything else will fall into place."

Jesus constantly put the emphasis on loving God, on adoring Him. Prior to this interaction with the Pharisees, in Matt. 6 and 7, we find Jesus wrapping up His famous Sermon on the Mount. If you read this block of Scripture and break it up as most modern Bibles do, separating it concept per concept with the subject headings, it's easy to miss the overall thought process Jesus follows. But if you read both books as a whole, it's easy to see that Matt. 6—7 is about loving God with all your heart, soul, and mind. Matt. 6:31-33 encapsulates the whole idea: "So do not worry, saying, 'What shall we eat?' or 'What shall we drink?' or 'What shall we wear?' For the pagans run after all these things, and your heavenly Father knows that you need them. But seek first his kingdom and his righteousness, and all these things will be given to you as well" (NIV).

Jesus doesn't say to make God the highest priority. In essence, He says God is the only priority. Loving Him and seeking His kingdom is all that matters. When we do that, God takes care of the rest.

WHERE IS THE LOVE?

My indictment against Christians is that we spend far less time simply falling in love with the majesty, wonder, and mystery of God than we should. We seem to be more concerned that our sins are forgiven, that we're "saved and sanctified for the work of the Lord," than that we don't spend nearly enough time resting in His presence. I believe when we're head-over-heals in love with God, all those issues fall into place.

Do we really believe that God created the whole universe? The compulsory answer is yes. But think about it. *Really* think about what that means. The power, the mind, the infinity necessary to conceive and put into motion all that exists, and then to hold it all in place is mind-boggling. If we accept at least portions of theories from modern chemistry and physics, the ability to create the unbelievable complexity of the cosmos is unfathomable.

Yet this same unfathomable power—this God—is the same power that calls us to simply know Him, thoroughly, completely, simply. He implores us, even begs us, "Come to Me. Know Me."

So why don't we flock to Him? Society finds itself irrevocably drawn to celebrity personalities. It's the association with them we crave. Somewhere around puberty the association with the cool crowd becomes a driving force in our lives. And the bigger the cool factor, the better. To be able to say that we know a celebrity personally is even more of a feather in our hats.

But where our spiritual walk is concerned, we don't think

of God as a celebrity. We aren't drawn to God as we are to famous humans. For whatever reason, the draw in knowing a famous human outweighs the draw of knowing the Creator of all that exists.

Loving God with all that we are, seeking Him with all that is within us takes guts, real guts. It means abandoning how we've approached God in the past. It means viewing Him in a different way for many, if not most, of us.

WHERE THE MIND IS

Famed poet and philosopher Ralph Waldo Emerson once said, "A man is what he *thinks* about all day long." He was right. The brain is the most complex and powerful organ in the body. It is the control center for the body, not only governing the biological functions but also coordinating the body's mental capacities. And the mind has an overwhelming influence over the moral and spiritual direction a body takes. There is an enormous catalog of scientific evidence indicating that when we spend a great amount of time focusing on a particular subject, it affects every part of who we are.

Ever heard the old saying "garbage in, garbage out"? The deeper meaning is if we fill our brains with junk, then what comes out of us will be junk as well. Very few would disagree with that little statement. But the opposite can be true as well. When we fill our minds with what is good and wholesome, that will be reflected in our actions, our speech, and our life.

Before there was any scientific evidence to back up this ideology, the apostle Paul challenged the Body of Believers in the city of Philippi to guard their minds as well. His challenge to the Philippians, as he closed his letter to them, was to focus their thoughts on all that was pure, noble, good, and praiseworthy. This same theme is reflected in Scripture from the beginning to the end. Guard your minds.

Unfortunately, popular civilization, our materialistic culture, and our oversexed society don't drive humanity to live in a manner that is wholesome and uplifting. In fact, it's just the opposite. One doesn't have to go far to see it either. Turn on the television or open up a newspaper or a popular magazine and you will be deluged with stories and images that are anything but uplifting to the mind and spirit. The books we read, the movies we watch, and the games we play are laced with violence, promiscuous sex, and debauchery. According to the American Academy of Pediatrics, studies confirm that there is a direct link between exposure to violence in the media and aggressive behavior. They report that by the time a child is 18 years old, he or she will have been exposed to over 200,000 acts of violence on the television alone.[5] Another report the academy offers reveals that each year Americans are exposed to over 14,000 sexually explicit images through both movies and television.[6] So in a situation where we just can't get away from such influence, it isn't a wonder that we struggle with focusing on what is wholesome.

In the midst of this, the Father calls us to focus on Him. If our minds are filled with the noise and background matter of all that wars against the kingdom of heaven, it's a safe bet we won't hear God when He speaks. Otherwise, like Elijah in the cave, we will be unable to recognize His presence in the whispering wind. Our minds will have been focused so long on what is destructive that we will mistake His presence for that of a violent tornado.

THE FINAL WORD

Our priorities are all screwed up. We've just got it all wrong. And because of this, we find ourselves coming to God daily, begging for His direction, wanting Him to answer our prayers, and curious why He doesn't. We've grown so used to the debauchery of the world that we fear the serenity of the Almighty.

And in the midst of that serenity, God's answer hasn't changed from the beginning:

> *You want your prayers answered? Change how you view Me and how you approach Me. Come to Me, please, come to Me. But first and above all, come to Me just to love Me, and to be loved by Me. And then forget about the rest. Let Me take care of the rest. But first, just come love Me.*

The gutsy question is, have you done that? If not, can you? And if you can't, quite honestly, you'll always struggle.

THOUGHT QUESTIONS

■ What do you think it means to delight yourself in the Lord?

- Can you honestly say that you delight in the Lord? If not, why?

- During your times with God, in addition to your quiet time just listening, how much time do you spend delighting in God?

- What changes in your spiritual walk would you need to make to begin loving God for the sheer joy of it? What obstacles stand in the way of you doing that?

- Do you view God as being a vengeful God or a loving God? If you see Him as vengeful, describe why.

BOLD AND COURAGEOUS

Scriptural Basis: *Read Josh. 1.*

To be sure, they were a ragtag bunch. From his vantage point on top of the hill, Joshua looked down across the masses of people gathered. Their ancient, tattered tent city fluttered in the light wind as people milled about in their daily routine. A dust devil swirled, rising in the distance in the growing heat of the day.

How long had it been? Forty years? Few remained who re-membered the days of captivity in Egypt, the brutality of their captors, and the incomprehensible manner by which God rescued them from their bonds of slavery. Now they were on the verge of entering the land promised to their fore-fathers, and Joshua would be the one to lead them into it.

A pang of nervousness stirred inside him. For the longest time it had been Moses leading their people. But now Moses was gone, and God had called Joshua to guide their nomadic people. Nomadic, yes, but not for long. Tomorrow they would cross the Jordan, and that would mark the be-ginning of their taking control of the land.

The pressure of leadership was nothing new to Joshua. Af-ter all, he had apprenticed under Moses for years. Even so, never had he been the one interpreting God's will. Always it had been Moses who spoke for God. Now he would serve in that capacity.

Joshua found it interesting how clearly God spoke to him. It hadn't been the first time in his life. It just seemed differ-ent somehow. *Be strong, and courageous!* God had told him. At least that was not something he struggled with. All his life God had given him boldness and courage, even in the face of insurmountable odds. That was his gift, his talent, so to speak—courage. When others faltered, Joshua was at ease in the strength God embedded within him. He trusted the power of the Almighty with implicit confidence.

The challenge for him was the second part of God's com-mand to him: "Do not let this Book of the Law depart from your mouth; meditate on it day and night" (Josh. 1:8, NIV).

That would be the key to his leadership of the Israelites, to remain in the Word of the Lord.

He gazed out over the masses. Below, at his tent at the base of the low hill on which he now stood, Joshua could see the leaders of the tribes of Israel gathering, seeking his counsel on the everyday issues, on the critical issues, on the minor issues. How easy it was to allow himself to be swept up into the business of running their nation. Each day the problems grew bigger and more overwhelming. It seemed the steady stream of issues was never ending. Despite his courage, his heart faltered momentarily. He was a man of action, not a man of politics and policy making. Yet this was the job he'd been called to. How would he survive?

"Meditate on it day and night."

The words echoed in his mind. That was the key. That was the answer. He would not let his people down. But far more importantly, he would not let God down. God's command was to meditate on the Word, day and night. God would provide all the direction Joshua needed.

Joshua smiled. The problems of the day would wait. Right now he needed God. Right now he needed the Torah. It was time to dig into the Word of God.

━ ━ ━ ━ ━ ━ ━

In the Cold War hysteria of the early 1980s, Warner Brothers released the film *Firefox*. Produced by and starring in the movie was the reigning action-film king of the era, Clint Eastwood. Critics have long panned the film as being one of Eastwood's worst releases ever, citing dreadful special effects, overused plot and subplot themes, and mediocre acting as reasons not to waste your time viewing it.

Regardless of the film critics' nay-saying, the premise of the movie is intriguing, nonetheless. United States intelligence services have learned that archnemesis nation Russia has created a flying weapons system threatening the balance of power in the world. This new prototype plane bristles with weaponry, flies six times faster than the speed of sound, and operates by the mind control of its pilot. In response, the benevolent United States government opts to steal the plane before it can go into mass production, thereby halting the advance of this technology. Hence, Clint Eastwood's character—a retired, burned-out Vietnam veteran fighter pilot—is pressed back into service, as he is the only hope in the world for pulling off the mission and thereby assuring global peace.

Aside from the glaring plot flaws—the fact that theft will *not* halt the production and improvement of future renditions of this technology, and the fact that it's so drastically unlikely that the character played by Clint Eastwood would even be a candidate whom the U.S. government would seek to accomplish this mission—I still find the movie fascinating. It's the underlying technology that captivates me. You see, in order to fly the plane, the pilot has to know the Russian language. But beyond speaking Russian, because the plane's inner workings tap into the pilot's brain waves, the pilot actually has to think in Russian as well. Hence Eastwood's character is whisked to England for a crash course in Russian.

Smuggled into Russia and into the testing facility by indigenous military dissidents, Eastwood's character manages to steal the plane. And, as luck would have it, he is pursued by prototype No. 2. On not just one occasion during the heated aerial battle, Eastwood's character forgets to think in Russian when commanding the plane to respond, making the dog fights even more of a nail-biting cliff-hanger. In the end, Eastwood succeeds in his mission and the world is saved from certain disaster.

The success of the mission does not rely on the Eastwood character's skill as a pilot, nor on his ability to be cool under fire. It lies in his ability to *think* in another language. Otherwise, the plane would not respond to what he wants it to do.

THE SECRET TO HIS SUCCESS

Now consider what God was calling Joshua to do in Josh. 1. God's command wasn't a call for Joshua to just spend time with Him but to make God's written Word, the Law, so much a part of himself, by meditating on it day and night, that it would take over Joshua's thoughts and actually drive what came out of his mouth. God promised him, if he would imbibe his written Word to that extent, he would be prosperous and successful.

I also love the other part of what God tells Joshua: "Be strong and courageous. Do not be terrified; do not be discouraged, for the LORD your God will be with you wherever you go" (v. 9, NIV). In other words, have guts! God commands Joshua to have guts—to have the guts to be so deep in His Word that there would be no way Joshua could go wrong. He needed to trust that God would direct his every move. That level of intimacy takes raw guts.

But isn't that the call God lays on all of us? To have the guts to place our daily focus so much on Him and on His written Word that all other distractions are stripped away? Aren't we called to meditate on Him and His Word so deeply that we will actually begin thinking the thoughts of God? Not that we become God, mind you, but that our thoughts are those that He implants within us, within our context of living, within our families, friendships, and work affiliations.

When I was a single man living in Colorado Springs, I had one of the best roommates I've ever had in my life. His name was Cuby Valdez. The most notable trait about Cuby was that he was a terribly scatterbrained individual. He was always forgetting things: paying his phone bill, appointments he'd made, picking up his girlfriend from work, critical daily chores. One time we were cleaning out a storage closet and I came across a bag full of wrapped presents. I asked him if he knew anything about it. It was then that he realized the bag was full of all the presents he'd purchased for his nieces and nephews the previous Christmas! After a good laugh, I asked him if, or when, he realized he'd forgotten to take all his gifts when he flew to Los Angeles for their family's Christmas celebration. "Well, I remember thinking that something seemed like it was gone, but it just didn't dawn on me that it was all the presents for the kids. So I just went shopping again when I got there." I think he ended up donating those rediscovered gifts to Toys for Tots.

The most ironic thing about Cuby was that he knew more Scripture by heart than any other person I've ever known. He literally had entire books of the Bible committed to memory. Whenever I found myself in difficult circumstances, Cuby always had a brilliant block of Scripture he would quote to encourage me.

I once asked him how he could remember so much Scripture but couldn't remember from moment to moment if he'd put his shoes on before leaving for work. "When a person decides what their priorities in life are going to be, nothing will stop them from achieving them," he said. For Cuby, his priority was to know the Word of his Savior. He woke up every day, without fail, at 4 A.M. to read, memorize, and study the Bible. He spent no less than an hour each day digging into God's Word. Cuby had chosen his priority in life. Nothing would stop him from achieving it. Cuby was one of the most amazing individuals I've ever met. And God has used him in mighty ways, despite his absentmindedness.

That's the level of intimacy God wants with us as well. God has been seeking that level of intimacy with humanity since the fall of Adam and Eve. He has desperately been searching for those willing to commit to that deep of a spiritual relationship.

At that level of closeness, we always ask the right questions. At that proximity to God, it's difficult to go wrong. That's when having guts becomes second nature.

"Be strong and courageous." Have guts.

"Do not let this Book of the Law depart from your mouth; meditate on it day and night." Dedicate your life to knowing Me intimately, every day.

Understand, however, that level of commitment is easier said than done. That level of commitment takes real guts.

A MODERN-DAY JOSHUA

She wasn't flamboyant or charismatic by any stretch. To look at her a person never would assume he or she was standing in the presence of greatness. In fact, it was more likely she would be completely overlooked in a crowd. She was *that* unremarkable, physically speaking. Yet this small, demure woman had been chosen by God as one of modern times' foremost Christian leaders.

But she never thought of herself in that manner. She simply saw herself as nothing but an instrument to be used by the hand of God. If the Almighty called her to do nothing, she would do nothing. If God asked her to contact a world leader, she would. If she were moved by the Spirit to extend a cup of clean water to a prostitute, she would do so without question. In her opinion, she was but a servant. She touched lepers and prayed for them. She held the hands of diseased outcasts, wept with them as they hurt, laughed with them as they convalesced. She brought with her a message of forgiveness, a presence of love, a bastion of peace. This simple, small woman, this frail icon of strength, this Mother Teresa was a world changer.

What does it take to be a world changer? Judge for yourself. Consider the life of Mother Teresa. She was born into a modest Albanian family, with no real name or significant stature in the community to identify her as someone who would become great. As a teenager she felt God calling her into service, and so she became a nun in the Roman Catholic Church. She became a teacher of small children and while serving in that capacity contracted tuberculosis. Her diocese sent her to Darjeeling to rest and recover. On the train to Darjeeling she felt God calling her to Calcutta to minister to the poor and the outcasts. Understand, however, she had no credentials or notoriety to identify her as one who could even pull off such an undertaking. All she had was a calling. But she recognized and acted on that calling. Through her obedience over the years, God ministered to thousands of people who otherwise would have been overlooked and forgotten.

In a conference I attended a number of years ago, Lorrie Salerno was one of the keynote speakers. During her time on the stage, she spoke of her annual trips to Calcutta to work in the original mission established by Mother Teresa. Lorrie told of being overwhelmed as she was surrounded by the unending human need in Calcutta. She wondered how the mission was able to accomplish anything amid the overwhelming circumstances. When she inquired from one of the sisters how they did it all, the answer was that Mother Teresa spent an hour in prayer every morning.

"An hour in prayer?" Lorrie responded. "How does she have that much time to devote to prayer?"

The sister smiled at her and responded, "Lorrie, my child, how else would she make it through each day? When facing so much tragedy as we do on a daily basis, how could she not spend that much time with God? That is what Mother Teresa has always done."

Lorrie, impressed by the response, pressed for more. "An hour of prayer, and then what does she do?"

"What does she do?" the sister responded, a little confused. "What else would she do, Lorrie? After she prays, she obeys."

"That's it?"

"There is nothing else. She prays, and then she obeys."

COMPARE FOR YOURSELF

Mother Teresa spent hours each day praying, communing with her Creator. After her daily quiet times, she simply obeyed what God told her, no matter how insurmountable the odds might have been. As a result, she changed a nation without fighting, without violence, without political power.

The simplicity of such a response seems unbelievable, as if there has to be more. One would think there would be a gathering of the board members to discuss all the possibilities. Maybe there would be a vote or a collection of opinions. Maybe there would be a poll taken or prioritization of ministry possibilities. But that's not how it happened.

Nor does the Bible record that those things happened in Joshua's day. He simply spent time day and night with God. And when God directed him to do something, Joshua simply obeyed. There was no gathering of the board of directors. There was just action. It did not matter if the Israelite army seemed overwhelmed by the might of the opposing army. When God said attack, they did. They trusted God to work out the details. They simply obeyed without question.

Could it really be that simple? Pray and obey? How do we know we're doing the right thing? How do we know we won't be going down the wrong road?

Guts. Time with God, in His Word, always takes guts. It takes guts to obey what He communicates to us during those times. Maybe the reason why we don't have more world changers like Joshua and Mother Teresa is because so few of us are willing to meditate on the Word day and night, praying and then obeying.

THOUGHT QUESTIONS

- Do you see yourself in the same league as Joshua or Mother Teresa? Why or why not?

- Do you think it is possible for God to use you as a world changer in the same way that He used Joshua and Mother Teresa? Describe why you feel that way.

- How hard is it for you to obey the things God calls you to do? Is it difficult for you to obey after you pray?

TIME TO GO ON LIVING

Scriptural Basis: *Read John 18:1-13.*

The dark of the midnight closed in on Him, smothering Him, crushing Him. Faint tendrils of moonlight filtered through the stifling canopy of tree limbs above them, vaguely illuminating the surrounding ground and rock formations. There was no wind, no rustling sound of night creatures. Save for the deep breathing of those resting soundly on the ground around Him, a deep, foreboding silence gripped the night.

At His feet Jesus' friends dozed, too tired from the day's events to stay awake. He had twice begged them to stay awake and pray with Him. After the second time, knowing their eyes were too heavy to keep open, He simply allowed them to sleep. They really didn't understand what was at stake or what was about to happen. Bantering them to remain conscious was pointless.

Instead Jesus chose to spend those last peaceful moments of His mortal life alone with His Father. He had wept bitterly, knowing the anguishing path that lay ahead. Since before the existence of time Jesus had never known one fleeting moment away from the presence of His Heavenly Father. If they were to complete their plan, if salvation for the fallen race of Adam was ever to come, Jesus would have to become eternity's sacrificial lamb. The sins of all time would be heaped on Him, on the One who for all of eternity had never known sin. It wasn't the pain, the torture, or the scorn that Jesus feared. It was the sin. And when He would bear that sin, the Father who had always watched over Him with pride and love, would finally be forced to look away. It was that reality He almost could not bear. But it would have to be done in order to complete the plan. There was no way around it.

The Father encouraged Jesus, languishing all of himself on His Son, encouraging Him that it would only be a short time. Jesus filled himself with the Father's presence, reveling in the ultimate freedom, encouraged by the ecstasy of the Infinite.

He had come to the garden, knowing the answers to His questions in the first place. *If there is another way, God, let's go that way. But more than anything, I want Your will to be done in My life. And if the only way to save humanity is for Me to take on the sins of all time, then that's what I want to do.*

The time had come. The plan was set. He had His answers. Their plan to save humanity was still on course. Without any further hesitation, Jesus ended their time of communion. No more delays. No more tears. No more questions or regrets.

He'd prayed for God's will to be done. He'd asked the right questions. Then He bravely faced His destiny, knowing His prayer *would* be answered and three days hence, sin would be conquered forever.

The sound of footfalls in the distance pierced the wretched silence. They were coming. It was time to fulfill His calling.

— — — — — — —

Obedience is hard. Often obedience means risking rejection, certain loss, and even life itself. Obedience is the gutsy part of the whole equation. Obedience is the key to God's will being fulfilled on earth as it is in heaven.

It comes down to that in the end. We can pray for hours. We can search the Word of God from cover to cover. We can seek the counsel of others until we've heard every opinion that exists. God could even speak to us audibly. But unless we are willing to take that final step, all the seeking is pointless. We must act.

From the previous chapter, I love what God promises Joshua

after telling him to spend time in the written Word day and night. The answer isn't to keep waiting for another answer. The answer is to be bold, be brave, be courageous. Without regret, Joshua is to move forward. God promises Joshua He'll reveal to him what His will is. God doesn't tell Joshua He'll keep him guessing forever. No. God's promise is to reveal what His plans are. After that, Joshua was to move forward with them with boldness, with guts. God hasn't changed. He still makes the same promise today. The promises He made to Joshua are the same promises He makes to you and me and to His people everywhere.

I love the boldness, the resolve with which Jesus moved forward with the task ahead of Him in John 18. He knew what was to happen. He knew that Judas would betray Him to the chief priests. When they came to the garden looking for Him, carrying torches and armed to the teeth, rather than running away Jesus went out to meet them. And when He informed them He was the one they were looking for, His confidence was such that they fell to the ground, struck down by fear of the power He engendered.

Isn't it great that, after they are struck silly by His self-assurance, He asks them again who they are looking for. It was almost as if He wanted to make sure they were up to the underhanded task they had come to pull off. He did not delay His purpose one moment longer. He stepped right up to it, doing all He could to get it underway, confident in what the ultimate outcome would be.

Obviously, we are not quite the same as Jesus. While Jesus knew exactly what would happen to Him, we may not understand how everything will work out in the beginning. In fact, more than likely there will be times when what He's called us to do seems impossible. But we can be confident that God does know the outcome, and He will not fail us. That is the fact we must rely on. And in the same way that Jesus faced the Cross, we must face the tasks we are confronted with.

We are not called to work out everything. We are simply called to be obedient. It is God's job to work out what is impossible. And He has quite a bit of experience working out such details.

THOUGHT QUESTIONS

▪ When obeying the call God places on you, do you find yourself trying to figure out the details first?

▪ Does working out the details stop you from acting?

▪ Do you find it difficult to trust that God will work out the details of what He calls you to do? Why or why not?

LIVING
THE
DREAM

Scriptural Basis: *Read Gen. 41.*

18

What happened to the dream? he wondered. *How can a ruler of nations come from the depths of a dungeon?*

Joseph stared up at the cold ceiling, wondering what he had ever done to deserve this. Exactly what sin had he committed to be subjected to such injustice? In the rotting filth of a forgotten prison he lay on a makeshift rag bed he'd created, wondering if he'd ever see freedom again. It was doubtful. He had no allies outside of the prison walls. No one with any influence that could help even knew he existed. Without that, it was virtually impossible for him to ever see freedom again.

Years ago he'd been hated, beaten, and sold into slavery by his own brothers, all because of their jealousy over the attention their father showed to him. He hadn't chosen to be his father's favorite. He had not campaigned for it or done anything in particular. His brothers just hated him, and so they acted, kidnapping him and selling him to slave traders, as if he were a piece of livestock.

After being transported to Egypt, he was sold off to the highest bidder, a high-ranking official named Potiphar. There was nothing he could do but apply himself to the situation dealt to him. His devotion to God and strength of character would not allow him to give anything but his best to the responsibilities given him. So he did. And everything he touched was blessed. Potiphar realized that early on and soon put Joseph in charge of the household.

But as luck would have it, while Potiphar was a man of character himself, his wife was not. She sought to have her way with Joseph, to have relations with this slave of their household. Naturally, Joseph refused, choosing instead to steer clear of her. But as a slave, and with his limited freedom, his refusals in her eyes were interpreted as insults. The final time he refused she falsely accused him of rape. So Potiphar threw Joseph into prison—the one he now called home.

Yet through everything, he still had his dreams. As a young teenager he'd dreamed God would make him the ruler of a nation. Even his own family would bow down to him. Joseph grunted to himself, certain it was impossible for those dreams to come true now. No one with the power to free him even knew who or where he was. Sometimes he even wondered if God had forgotten him. But then he caught the direction his thoughts were going. Steeling his nerves, refusing to allow doubt or bitterness any foothold, he reminded himself that God had big plans for him. He believed it. His gut told him so. He chose to hold on to the dreams despite his impossible circumstances.

Joseph roused, forcing himself to get up. Even in prison he had responsibilities. Somehow God had blessed him even here. Over the years of his stay in this rotting dungeon, the jailer realized that Joseph could be trusted—so much so that the jailer placed him in charge of the entire prison. Joseph had his daily duties to attend to. At least that gave him something to concentrate on to take his mind off his hopeless situation.

Joseph exited the alcove he called his room and almost ran headlong into the warden. The man was flanked by two stout Egyptian royal guards, worry and dread painted all over his face.

"What is the trouble," Joseph asked, "that you would come here at this early hour?"

The warden licked his lips and cleared his throat. "These guards have been sent for you, Joseph," he stated. "It's Pharaoh. He's sent for you."

Joseph nodded, uncertain what business the ruler of Egypt might have with an imprisoned slave. He realized he had not dressed yet. Feeling exposed and uncertain, he said, "I'll get my robe."

"No," the warden said, shaking his head, "there's no time. These guards are here to take you now. Pharaoh has not rested all night long. They will take you to be cleaned and dressed before you are brought before our lord."

Joseph nodded, reading the concern in his unlikely friend's face. He would not argue. He would go now, as he was directed. One of the soldiers gripped his arm firmly, dragging him from where he stood and thrusting him into the corridor leading to the prison exit.

His mind raced, trying to comprehend what he might have done. He could not fathom why Pharaoh would seek an audience with him. Could this be related in any way to what happened in Potiphar's house all those many years ago? He doubted it. He vaguely remembered a time many years before when he'd asked Pharaoh's cupbearer, who had been temporarily imprisoned, to put in a good word for him when he got out. After so many years it was unlikely that that request had finally been honored. There seemed to be no explanation, but whatever it was, it certainly would not be good. Doom engulfed him.

Later that day, some 40 years after he first received his dream from God, Joseph became the ruler of Egypt. Only Pharaoh was above him. God made the impossible possible.

— — — — — — —

No, God hadn't forgotten Joseph. He was just setting the stage for what the world would call unbelievable. God planned to save nations from starvation through the dreams and interpretations of an imprisoned slave. And that's exactly what God did. Almost 40 years after giving the dreams to Joseph—that's right, 40 years—God brought the dream to fruition, moving Joseph from the depths of a prison to the throne of a kingdom in one day.

We have such a short-minded view of reality. In our instant-access, instant-food, instant-information world, we've lost sight of what it means to wait. The idea that we might have to wait on God to work out the details of His plans is foreign to us. We have no patience. Unfortunately, God's timing is usually much slower than ours.

We've simply lost sight of what it means to wait on the Lord. We find it hard to believe that God would even have a plan or a dream for our lives as well. God has always had a dream for His people. But due to impatience, insecurity, personal short-sightedness, or a variety of other reasons, we often lose sight of this fact. Maybe we think we're too old or too young. Maybe we think we don't have the skill set or the charisma to do the job. Or quite possibly, maybe we've never really thought that God might have a dream for us.

What about you? Do you believe that God has a dream for your life? It's true. He really does. And even if you haven't spent the time with God I've challenged you to spend with Him throughout this book, I'm willing to guess He's already whispered His dream to you.

Why do I believe this? Because God has never wanted to keep His plans for us silent. It's not His desire to keep us guessing. While He doesn't always reveal all the details of what He will do or how He will work out His plan, the narrative of the Bible, from cover to cover, shows how God has always wanted His people to know what He will do for them and through them.

It's our own hang-ups that keep us from grabbing hold of what God might have for us. But when we're willing to throw caution to the wind, to become completely obedient—to have guts—trusting God to work out the details, God is willing and able to turn misfits into world changers. He's been doing that throughout history.

THEY ALL HAD GUTS

It might be difficult for you to believe that God uses misfits to change the world. If you don't, take a look at this lineup of who God has used in building His kingdom:

- As a young man, he lost control of himself when he saw another of his countrymen being beaten by a guard. As a result, he killed the guard in defense of his fellow citizen and ended up as a fugitive. On the other end of the spectrum, he also had a speech impediment. Speaking in front of people was one of his mortal fears. It didn't matter to God though. God called this man to lead his people, the Israelites, out of slavery. He was a murderer, a fugitive, his name was Moses, and he was a misfit.

- She was the grand madam of one of the leading brothels in her city. She was one of the most unlikely candidates to become a leading figure in the lineage of Jesus, the Christ. Yet her faith in God and her willingness to be used as an instrument to establish the nation of Israel distinguished her name, saved her family, and won her the right to be an ancestor of the Son of God. She was a prostitute, a madam, her name was Rahab, and she was a misfit.

- Their nation had been crushed, and they were all prisoners, slaves to a conquering nation. Who would think they had any power to make a difference. Yet their devotion to God and unswerving resolve to live according to their beliefs almost cost them their lives. But it also caused a self-centered King Nebuchadnezzar to pause, to recognize the power of God, and to call his nation to repent of their sins. They were exiles, prisoners, their names were Shadrach, Meshach, Abednego, and Daniel, and they were misfits.

- He was a self-centered swindler, willing to do whatever it took to get what he felt was coming to him. He'd cheated his oldest brother out of the inheritance that was due him, by disguising himself and lying to his near-blind father. He played favorites with his kids, too, causing severe jealousy to arise between them. Yet despite all that, he loved God, and as a result, his 12 sons became the 12 tribes of Israel. He was a cheater, a poor example of a father, his name was Jacob, and he was a misfit.

- He was nobody. He was a poor rancher's son, the youngest of all his brothers and the least likely in his time to amount to anything. Nothing ever went to the youngest son. But he loved God with a passion. And he had bravery beyond compare. He was also a musician and poet and was completely willing to be used by God in whatever way He chose. God chose to make him the king of Israel. He was poor, too young to be usable by normal standards, his name was David, and he was a misfit.

- She was a nobody, literally a nobody. The only thing she had going for her was that her poor parents had found a good man with a good business to betroth her to. Oh, and she loved God, with a passion. Then one day she found herself pregnant out of wedlock, and this despite the fact that she was still a virgin. The Law declared that she should have been stoned to death for her condition. She was a nobody, pregnant out of wedlock, the mother of Jesus, her name was Mary, and she was a misfit.

- They were passed over has-beens. They had received their fair shake in the leadership of their countrymen, having been raised in the traditional Jewish way. As was the custom, they had all studied under a rabbi at some time. But all had been passed over, not good enough to go through additional training in order to eventually become rabbis themselves and then move into Jewish leadership. Instead they'd been sent back home to apprentice under their respective family businesses. They were fishermen, taxmen, nobodies, and they'd been that for so long that the dream of becoming anything of importance had long passed them. So when this new rabbi, Jesus, came calling on them, it was not only countercultural but also unheard of. They were passed over has-beens, with no hope of being anything but common, they were the disciples, and they were misfits.

183

- He was a bounty hunter, certainly respected among some crowds. But he'd also been responsible for the beatings, mutilations, tortures, and even deaths of countless Christians. He was so notorious that his reputation preceded him wherever he went. He justified all that he was doing for the sake of protecting God's kingdom. One day God met him face-to-face and changed his entire life. As a result, this deadly executioner became the leading apostle in the Early Church, and through him, God changed the world. He was a bounty hunter, he was a dangerous threat, his name was Saul, and he was a misfit.

The common threads that run through the lives of each of the above individuals is that they loved God, they were willing to be used, and they all had the guts to be obedient when God called them. None of them were really cut out for the calling God placed on them. Sure, each had traits that might be lent to some form of leadership. But in almost all the cases, the odds were stacked against them ever being leaders by societal standards.

I believe that is often why we don't allow God to have His way with us, why we sometimes lack the guts to allow God to move us forward into the dreams He has for us. Our current circumstances make it impossible for us to believe God would or could use us. We allow our circumstances to steal our guts.

IT WRAPS UP LIKE THIS

Consider the dreams and outrageous plans God may be calling you to. It doesn't matter whether or not you think you're qualified. It doesn't matter whether or not you think you're worthy. God wants to use His people in mighty ways. He just wants them to have guts about it. Guts to believe the dream. Guts to hang on to the dream. Guts to move forward with the dream.

The question is, if God spoke to Joseph, Mary, Saul, and countless other misfits throughout history, challenging them to grab hold of the dream, why would He change how He operates now? The answer is, He wouldn't. He just wants His people to believe the dream He has for them and to press forward toward that goal, with a faith that has guts.

By now, hopefully, you have a better understanding of what it takes to have a faith with guts. It's not really a 12-step plan. It's not a formulaic approach by any stretch. And what might work for some might not work at all for others. If there's anything from this book that resembles a formula, it might be this:

A faith that has guts means:

- You understand that God has a calling on your life, a calling He wants you to move toward no matter how crazy it might seem.

- Prayer is critical to have a faith with guts. But prayer time with God is more than a laundry list of requests; it's also a whole lot of listening to the Spirit of God as He speaks to our hearts.

- Spending time in the written Word of God is another critical part of hearing God's call on our life, and it's also critical for confirming what our hearts are saying to us.

- Obedience in the call is a principal factor. And trusting that God will work out the details is a must. Otherwise, fear and self-doubt will hinder the work of God.

With these final "thought questions," I challenge you to release what fears you may have, what insecurities might be holding you back from a gutsy moving forward with God's plan for your life. May God richly bless you with courage and peace, as He moves you ever closer to claiming the outrageous dream He has for you.

THOUGHT QUESTIONS

- Write down your wildest dreams for your life in the context of the kingdom of God.

- Do you see God moving you in the direction of fulfilling that dream? Do you believe that dream is God-given or self-motivated?

- What barriers stand in the way of those dreams being achieved? What would God need to do in order for those dreams to be fulfilled?

■ Examine your dreams. Are they in alignment with what the Bible teaches? With the character, will, and nature of God? If not, are you willing to let go of these dreams so God can give you new ones?

NOTES

1. Rabbi Aryeh Kaplan, *The Handbook of Jewish Thought* (New York: Maznaim Publishing Corporation, 1979), 13.

2. Albert Truesdale, *If God Is God, Then Why? Letters from Oklahoma City* (Kansas City: Beacon Hill Press of Kansas City, 1997), 82.

3. Ibid., 91.

4. Susie Shellenberger, *Stuff You Don't Have to Pray About* (Nashville: Broadman and Holman, 1995), vii-viii.

5. "Some Things You Should Know About Media Violence and Media Literacy," http://www.aap.org/advocacy/childhealthmonth/media.htm, August 27, 2005.

6. "Pediatrician Presents Findings That Sexually Explicit Media Has Significant Impact on Children," http://www.aap.org/advocacy/washing/sex_in_media.htm, August 27, 2005.

An honest look at the frustration of waiting . . .

it's about time.

Examine the mysteries of God's timing and learn to transform the frustration of waiting into a positive force that will enrich and change your life.

When God Takes Too Long
Learning to Thrive During Life's Delays
By Joseph Bentz

ISBN-13: 978-0-8341-2218-5

Available wherever Christian books are sold.